TwiLite

STEPHEN JENNER

Cover design by Michael Lado.

This book is a work of fiction. Any resemblance to actual events or persons, living or dead, is entirely coincidental.

This book is a parody and has not been prepared, approved, or authorized by the creators or producers of the "Twilight" series.

"TwiLite," by Stephen Jenner. ISBN 978–1-60264–381-9.

Manufactured in the United States of America.

For Lynn and Michael

"Beware the Jabberwock, my son!
The jaws that bite, the claws that catch!
Beware the Jubjub bird, and shun
The frumious Bandersnatch!"

- Lewis Carroll, from *Jabberwocky*

PREFACE

I'M QUITE CERTAIN that I am going to die today. If I were a betting man, I'd let it all ride on red—*blood red*—that I'll get ripped limb from limb in just a few minutes.

But let's face it—I've been dying a slow death living in this godforsaken hellhole of a town these past several months. I gave up Phoenix with its eternal sunshine, palm trees, and strip malls for *this*? Do I have regrets? Hell, yeah!

For a brief shining moment, I have to stop and think of how my life has changed by coming to Sporks. How my hopes and dreams have been fulfilled beyond anything I could possibly have imagined. How, you ask? Well, I just saved a bunch of money on my truck insurance by switching to Geico. I kid, I kid.

Back to what's happening here. Standing before me is a particularly disturbing guy with long, pointy fangs who invited me over for lunch, and I'm the main course. I sure hope he fills up on appetizers.

1. IT'S ALL ABOUT ME

"CALL ME AS SOON AS YOU GET THERE," my mother told me. She had just pulled the car into the drop-off area near the airport's terminal for departing flights and lovingly nudged me out the door. She then tossed me an apple to take on the plane, but that slipped through my fingers and splattered as it hit the ground. I grabbed my one suitcase containing my entire life's belongings, gave mom a peck on the cheek, and watched her drive away. My days in Phoenix were thus coming to an end. Fortunately, my dad, "Clueless" Harley Crow, was welcoming me into his home. Unfortunately, he lived in the gloomiest, dankest, darkest area of the country: Sporks, Washington.

Call me Stella. I'm a seventeen year old girl of average height and the athleticism of a dyslexic hermit crab. I tend to fall down a lot, but only if I've been standing immediately prior to this. Apart from for the occasional game of roller derby or full contact bingo, I avoid sports at all costs. My clumsiness has never really been problem for me—it's not like I'm running from a pack of werewolves or a gaggle of vampires all the time.

I spent my entire life here in Phoenix, and would gladly have stayed at least through high school. But this was not meant to be. My mother, who works at the local circus as a sideshow freak and is proudly known as "The largest woman in the Greater Phoenix/Tri-State area," recently met and fell in love with a professional badminton player. Bill Mancini, known on the professional circuit as "The Beast" (a name that would be fitting for mom as well) met my mother at a Denny's all-you-can eat breakfast, lunch and dinner buffet, and the two immediately fell head over heels for one another. One month later they were married, and together they lovingly kicked me out of the house. Hence, my premature exile from the Grand Canyon State. My new life in the Great Northwest would begin in just a matter of hours.

———   ——   ———

"How was your flight, Stella?" Harley asked as he greeted me at the baggage carousel at Sporks International Airport. He picked up my over-stuffed suitcase and placed it in my right hand. I guess he decided that I would be the one to lug it to the car. Ah Harley, always the gentleman.

"It was fine, Harley—I mean, *dad*." I said.

A bashful smile came to Harley's face. "Wow…*dad*. I haven't heard you call me that in ten years." Harley said nostalgically.

For a few moments Harley was in deep thought, which was something he avoided like the plague. After blinking his eyes several times he turned to me and said, "To be quite honest, I'm not sure I'm too crazy about you calling me 'dad.' How about you call me 'Police Chief Harley, King of the Universe,' or 'Doctor Dread, Peace Officer,' or better yet, 'O captain, my captain!?"

"Maybe we should just stick with 'Harley' for now," I suggested, hoping that this would end the discussion before it got even more ridiculous. Harley nodded, and then tossed a green M&M into his mouth.

I followed Harley to the airport parking lot. To my surprise, he walked up to a beautiful flaming red 2009 Corvette, reached in his pocket and pulled out a set of keys. He tossed them to me.

"Care to drive us home in *your* new car?" he asked trying to contain a smile.

"What? This is *my* car? Are you kidding me? I can't believe it! "

Harley's grin turned into an all out guffaw. "Yeah, I *am* kidding." Harley said. "I made a funny. Your new…*truck*…is over there."

I turned my head to locate the vehicle he was pointing to. The parking lot was mostly empty, and the only nearby vehicles were sedans and mini vans. Other than a run-down rusted heap of twisted metal that long ago might have resembled a pickup truck, there wasn't anything else you could call a "truck" in the lot.

"Here, let me put your luggage in the back for you," Harley said as he heaved my suitcase into the twisted lump of steel. "It's all yours, and already paid for. Consider it a housewarming gift. Got it from an old friend of mine. It's no spring chicken, and it ain't too pretty to look at, but it's certainly good enough for you."

"Thanks, Harley," I choked out not knowing how to respond. "That's, uh, that's really sweet of you, I think." Now *that's* Father of the Year material.

Harley hopped in the truck and turned on the ignition. After driving for nearly an hour, he finally found his way out of the parking lot. It really struck me then that I had not seen Harley since mom kicked him out of the house ten years ago after stealing one too many Twinkies from her private stash. The thing that I most remember about him, however, is this: He's an idiot, but a loveable one. He also happens to be the Sporks' Chief of Police ("I'm one damn fine cop, if you ask me," he would insist).

Harley earned his nickname "Clueless" because he had no idea of the things happening right around him. Hell, I could have mysterious visitors in my bedroom every other night and Harley would be completely clueless to this fact. I'm speaking hypothetically, of course. Fortunately for everyone, little was asked of Harley in this remote, quiet, ultra depressing, perpetually gloomy town. The limited capabilities that he did have were sufficient to run the local police force: It's not like there was daily gang violence between a family of vampires and a clan of adolescent boy-werewolves. Huh. I know that's a strange comparison but it just keeps coming to me for some reason. And if there were, in truth, he would also be completely oblivious to this. "I like pancakes!" he would announce to me at random moments. "And I have a gun. I shoot bad guys with it. Sometimes, bad guys go to sleep and don't wake up. That makes Harley sad." Bless his heart.

During our drive home, Harley told me about the pickup truck's previous owner. The truck had been owned by a boy named Yakob Brown, the son of Harley's oldest and dearest friend. Yakob lives with his dad on the other side of town and goes to a different school than where I would be going. Harley told me that Yakob was a real nice kid, but since he was a couple years younger than me and did not live close by we'd probably never be friends. Anyway, Yakob was some kind of gifted mechanic and kept the truck running long after it should've been given up for dead. What a lucky gal I am.

After a thirty-minute drive that included several stops to add oil to the engine, we arrived at Harley's home. I lugged my suitcase up the stairs and Harley opened the front door. Before I entered the house Harley told me that he had spent the entire week fixing up the place for my arrival. I thanked him, and then walked inside. In a nutshell, his house was fit for a swine. I blinked back tears from the stench. I was sure that some vermin came to Harley's living room to die. Cigarette cartons, empty bottles of whiskey, and *Where's Waldo* books were strewn about the house like this place had been hit by a tornado over and over again. But Harley was grinning his wide just short of a six-pack grin. He actually seemed quite pleased with how the house looked. I knew that if I were to live here, this simply would not do. So I spent the entire evening straightening up, draining old whiskey bottles, wrapping up carcasses in old towels and putting them in large Hefty bags, and trying to get KFC grease stains out of the carpet. I actually managed to make the place look respectable. I knew in my heart, though, that in twenty-four hours the house would again look terrifying.

Harley seemed quite pleased that I was now staying with him. When he walked by me in his Scooby-Doo pajamas and matching slippers he gave me a warm smile and a gentle kiss on my forehead. Then he paused an extra moment to look at me as if he were seeing me for the very first time.

"I've never noticed it before, but you look so much like your mother when I married her," he said nostalgically. "She was like a beautiful angel with long, flowing hair and more layers of fat than I thought was humanly possible. She would make the cutest little grunting noises when I rubbed her belly. When she kissed me I was in hog heaven. We were so happy; I thought it would never end. But, in the end she had to follow her dreams. What man could compete with the calling of the circus freak show? Not this man, that's for sure."

"You never stood a chance, Harley," I said.

Harley slowly shook his head and started walking to his room. He suddenly stopped, and turned to face me. "Hey Stella, do you think you can gain a few hundred pounds and not shave your legs for months at a time? It would sure be nice to have someone looking like your mother around here again."

"Not a chance, pop," I said. I looked at him with no expression on my face. Harley was staring at me like a small boy would look at a parent holding his wrapped birthday gift. I slowly shook my head from side to side and said, "I didn't get Mom's genes, Harley. I just can't eat Crisco out of the can with a spoon and not gag."

Harley shrugged. "You can't blame a guy for trying. Good night, Stella. Good night, moon. Good night tiny mouse holding a green balloon."

2. BACK TO SCHOOL

THE NEXT MORNING I managed to fight off the scores of rabid cockroaches for the remaining morsels of Frosted Flakes. Harley was still in bed when I headed off to school. The day before he had told me that he planned to watch an all night marathon of "SpongeBob SquarePants." I'm sure that he did not get more than a couple hours of sleep. I remembered that Harley needed at least twelve hours of sleep each night or he'd be a zombie for the rest of the day. I was not about to interrupt his beauty sleep.

I got in my truck and managed to find my way to my new school. I turned down the tree-lined road leading toward the main building, and quickly noticed that the grounds of Prozac High School were immaculate. Every blade of grass seemed to be in its proper place, and each tree was full of healthy, green leaves. The pavement was freshly washed and sparkling clean. The birds sang together in sweet harmony, as if each note was carefully orchestrated by a musical director who spoke bird. Each building was an architectural masterpiece, one that Frank Lloyd Wright would have envied, or the Wright Brothers would have been honored to fly over. And I can personally vouch that every one of the two dozen Jiffy Johns that lined the hallways smelled minty fresh, and all had two-ply tissue paper, not the ultra thin onion skin that I grew up with. I knew that this place was something special.

As I walked the halls trying to find my first class I couldn't help but be in awe of the student body. With few exceptions, the students at Prozac High were exquisitely striking in their appearance. It was as if each had jumped off the cover of *Teen Magazine*: flawless skin, long eyelashes, high cheek bones, lustrous hair, and long, shapely legs. And I'm just talking about the boys. The girls were even *more* attractive. If I were to enter a beauty contest I could never keep up with them in the evening gown or swimsuit competition; but I could more than hold me own on questions about world peace. I got me some pretty good smarts in this head of mine.

My first day at school turned out to be rather eventful. I got the predictable stares a student would get starting at a new school. Word had also gotten around that I was Police Chief Harley's daughter, and most seemed rather surprised that some woman seventeen years ago willingly conceived a child with him. With all the attention I was beginning to feel a little like a circus sideshow freak—kind of like mom, just a few hundred pounds lighter. Nonetheless, I managed to meet some kids who seemed nice, and one of them, a pretty girl named Maria, invited me to have lunch with her. I thought that was very kind, and we agreed on a meeting time and place. I was particularly pleased because she seemed to be one of the more popular girls in school. Maybe a little of that would rub off on me.

Maria and I met up in the cafeteria at the beginning of lunch and immediately hit it off. I learned that she was half Spanish/half Italian and multilingual, but nonetheless took these same foreign language courses to boost her grade point average. Smart girl. She was also able to give me some inside information about other kids in school—the ones I needed to mingle with, and those I needed to avoid. I particularly appreciated that information, because I didn't want to get in with a bad crowd. It would certainly reflect badly on Harley if I were to run through the streets naked after an all night kegger. I wasn't about to let *that* happen again.

I was just about to start cleaning up the remains of my lunch when I looked across the cafeteria and first noticed them. A family of teenage boys and girls huddled together at a single table, far removed from the other students. I heard that they had come together from broken families, but these circumstances were unknown to nearly everyone at the school. The siblings clearly seemed to enjoy each other's company, and each actively participated in the lively conversations. Sometimes they talked together as a group, and other times they conversed with their same aged sibling.

These kids were all nicely dressed, well mannered and otherwise pretty much indistinguishable from the other students. The boys all had short, dark hair. The eldest and tallest boy seemed to be the one in charge. The middle boy was bellowing a song about going through changes, and not the least bit concerned that his painful singing would have made 1960's heartthrob Davy Jones turn in his grave. The girls, in stark contrast, were all blond, the youngest one in curls. The eldest girl had a visibly swollen nose that was the result of a domestic sports injury. But it was the middle girl who was most vocal, and certainly most agitated: "Marsha, Marsha, Marsha!" she cried out, her frustrations clearly broadcast across the cafeteria. I did not understand the nature of her displeasure, but I had this sense that it was a reoccurring theme, perhaps once a week, Friday nights at 8:00 p.m. eastern/7:00 central time. Those Brady kids seemed like one wacky bunch; I can only imagine what their 25-year reunion would be like.

Sitting at a separate table far away from the Brady bunch was a completely different family. I'll call them the Sullens, because that is their surname. And, as a matter of foreshadowing, I'm going to be referring to them for the next hundred pages quite often, so pay attention now, or you'll be *completely* confused from this point on. I can't stress this enough, people. And let me just say this: They were nothing—*nothing*—like the Bradys. Sony to Cher, Cain to Abel, Obama to McCain, Matthew McCaughnahey to *anyone* who can legitimately act. The point I'm trying to make is that they are really quite opposite families.

The Sullen kids looked nothing like each other, except for the fact that they all had darkish eyes and pointy teeth. Okay, they all had their limbs intact as well. They were an amazingly attractive clan, really good looking. And as beautiful as the girls were, the guys were the real *hotties*: Each one of them could be a model, right off the pages of *GQ* or *Weekly Reader Magazine*. A girl like me probably wouldn't stand much of a chance landing a stud like them. My gentleman callers more closely resembled the cover boys of *PRICK*, the international magazine for tattoo enthusiasts. But still, you can't keep a girl like me from dreaming.

Maria caught me staring over at the Sullen family and rolled her eyes. She seemed to know a little bit about them, or at least as much as anyone else around here. I decided to tap her brain.

"What's up with these Sullens anyway?" I asked her. "What's their story? Give me the scoop, would ya? Inquiring minds want to know."

Maria finished woofing down her chimichanga and quesadilla, took a shot of tequila, and turned her attention to me. "The five Sullen kids were all adopted by Dr. Sullen, the town physician, veterinarian and certified auto mechanic. Some of the kids are biological siblings. I think the boys. They just moved down here from Alaska. That's a state, but not part of the continental United States. It became part of the USA in 1959. Anyway, they pretty much keep to themselves. No one knows much more beyond that."

"Hmmm, interesting," I said.

I found myself staring at the Sullens, unable to turn my gaze away from them. One of the boys immediately caught my eye. He was tall and muscular. An exquisite being, a perfect form. A thing of beauty, a joy forever. I could imagine living the rest of my life with him—getting married when we were both in our mid to late thirties, having a normal baby boy after a full term pregnancy, and living in the big city among other mortals like ourselves. Unable to take my eyes off him, I asked Maria about this particular Sullen boy.

"What does a girl have to do to get a drink around here?" Maria shouted, slamming her empty shot glass on the table and staring ahead at nothing in particular.

"Maria, I'll buy you a drink later. But I need to know now who that boy is," I pleaded with her.

In her somewhat inebriated state Maria struggled to focus her eyes across the room. Nonetheless, she was able to identify the Sullen boy who had my full interest.

"Oh, yeah," she said. "I know who he is. His name is Casper. But he's taken; he's dating an older French girl from Transylvania. Or Pennsylvania. Something 'vania,' I can't remember which. Oh, and I'm pretty sure it's his sister."

Call me old fashioned, but that's just not right. So much for my perfect life.

I continued to scan the Sullens table for another available stud and quickly found one who was nearly as hot as Casper. Again I queried Maria, this time about the youngest Sullen boy, trying to hide my newly-formed schoolgirl crush on him.

"The boy over there, with the perfect face, nose, eyes, and lips...and chiseled chin, broad shoulders, strapping chest and tree trunk arms...and that V-shaped torso, thin waist and muscular legs like that of an Olympic cyclist. And perfectly manicured finger and toenails. Who is he, and what's his story?"

"Oh, that's Edweird," she said, rolling her eyes as if they were the seven and ten pins teetering and deciding whether to fall down or not. "He's dreamy. But he doesn't date. Apparently, even the best looking girls in the school are not good enough for him. Rumor has it that he's only interested in five foot four, average looking dark haired girls who only recently moved to Sporks from a hot climate state beginning with the letter "A." Go find someone who fits *that* description!" Maria dejectedly shook her head, the contents of her shot glass riding up and spilling over the sides. She leaned down close to the table, shot out her pink tongue and lapped up the droplets.

I now turned my full attention to Edweird. Edweird looked as though he was transplanted to Sporks from the pages of Greek mythology. He was tall, with long, lean muscles, perfect angular features, and boyish good looks—remarkably like the boy who played Cedric Diggory in the *Harry Potter* movies, but with spiky hair. That's all I'm going to tell you about Edweird *now*, but don't you worry: I'll be describing his perfection from this point on every chance I get in four—count 'em, four—amazingly long (and expensive) books. And then I'll interject descriptions of his perfection during other occasions when it's completely unnecessary to do so. Here, let me give you an example: When I was young I had a dog that was hit by a car and died. It made me very sad. Edweird never had a dog; what he did have was this exquisitely perfect facial bone structure that is rivaled only by his amazingly perfect strapping chest. See? You'll get the picture, which I will gladly paint for you, over, and over, and over again. I just can't seem to help myself.

Edweird, who sensed that I had been staring at him, seemed uneasy. From across the room our eyes briefly met—not physically, but figuratively—but he quickly looked away. After a moment he stopped shooting spit balls at his brothers and glanced back at me. He then reloaded his straw and pointed it in my direction. I stared down the barrel of the straw, which led to his perfect lips and mouth, and tongue, and that flap of skin that dangles from the back of your throat. Epiglottis? That too was perfect. But just as quickly as he raised his straw, he lowered it, and warily turned away.

Just then the school bell rang announcing the end of lunch. I had to make a quick departure from the cafeteria to search for my next class, Advanced Placement Pig Latin. I gathered my belongings and headed for the school's language wing. I found the classroom in time, and when I entered I saw Edweird already sitting in the back row. His presence startled me. He looked my way, giving me a cold stare, the kind of look that one gets when it's cold outside, and they are staring at you. He had an odd expression on his face, much like the one I remember Harley had when I told him where babies come from. When he saw me his look turned unfriendly, unwelcoming, standoffish, unreceptive, intolerant, and rigid. Beyond that, I had this sense that he wasn't quite pleased to see me. I'm incredibly perceptive that way.

Right before class began Edweird got up from his desk and walked over to the pencil sharpener. As he passed, he gave me a quick stare, and I felt shivers go up my spine, and chills back down. His gaze was icy, hard, and piercing, like an icy hard object that was capable of piercing something. I then felt my limbs go numb, and I collapsed to the floor, violently striking my head on the corner of my desk. As I wiped the blood from my face I returned his look and was awestruck by his glorious eyes.

His eyes. It was if a thousand of the bluest oceans had condensed at the end of his ocular nerve. If I were a sailor, or a bar maid named Brandy who served sailors whiskey and wine, I would have drowned in their blueness. His lips. As supple and as perfectly scented as a baby's bottom; full, pouting, expressive, and slightly chapped so from a distance it sort of looked like he had a faint mustache. His skin was perfect, like a *Cover Girl* model wearing Estee Lauder makeup. His shoulders were broad, and perfect, like one of those unbelievably muscular chicks you see on the cover of *Muscle Magazine*, who, without question, has been shooting up illegal steroids. But still, you got to admire their physique, because you know that they spend a boatload of time in the gym. His arms. What's the word I'm looking for? Oh yes—perfect. His buns were forged from pure Bethlehem steel. A hunk of coal would be transformed into a perfect diamond should they find their way between those luscious cheeks. Oh, and he had perfect hair too. Really nice-like.

His choice of attire was also hard to ignore. Although it was still balmy outside, he was dressed in long black pants and a long sleeved, black buttoned down shirt. So were his shoes, and matching socks.

And if I'm not mistaken, I thought I spotted a black cape peeking out of his backpack. *Hmmmm*, I thought to myself. I do not recall Old Navy pushing this type of apparel. And wasn't it a little early to be trying out your Halloween outfit? But since we were far north of the equator and closer to the sun, I figured that time moved more quickly, so trick or treating was not that far away after all. It all made sense now.

"Hello," he said coolly as he passed and walked back to his desk. His blueberry eyes were gleaming down at me; his French vanilla teeth peeking behind those cherry red lips; his pectorals tenderly danced like ripe mangoes under his form-fitting shirt. I got this sudden urge for a fruit shake.

Class soon began, and the teacher had us all read Homer's "The Odyssey" written in its original Pig Latin. I found it difficult to focus on the assignment, however. My mind was racing from all that had happened today, and school was barely half over. So I mostly just stared down at the pages and tried to collect my thoughts. Before I knew it the class was over and everybody started rushing out of the room. Edweird was the last student to pass by my desk. Immediately after he walked out the door I grabbed my things and started to follow him down the hall. I honestly can't tell you why I was doing this, I just felt compelled to do so. I followed him for a minute, when he suddenly turned around and looked inquisitively into my face. I froze for a moment.

"Hi," I finally managed to say, feeling quite relieved that I was blessed with the gift of gab.

Stephen Jenner

Edweird patiently waited for me to say something else. The brief yet uncomfortable silence was broken by the school bell.

"I need to go," Edweird said. "My next class is advanced remedial biology, and I want to make sure I get my favorite microscope before someone else grabs it."

"No way!" I said. "My next class is also advanced remedial biology. What are the odds?"

I thought I noticed a slightly pained expression on his face. At first, I thought it was the vegetarian tacos and refried beans they served for lunch, but then I remembered that Edweird hadn't eaten a thing. Before I could further examine his expression, he was gone.

I suddenly had mixed feelings about Edweird being in my class. On one hand, I felt compelled to learn more about him—maybe immerse myself into his entire being, get to know every atom of him, and then go out for some ice cream. On the other hand, I didn't need the distraction that would take my focus away from my work. There was no way I was going to fail a high school science class—not for a third time, that is.

By the time I found my way to the classroom every chair was occupied, save for the one next to— guess who—Edweird. I walked over to the lab table with my head down and sat next to him. I then gave him a quick look that was so fast there was no way he could have noticed it.

"I saw that," he said.

Damn.

"Can we just get started on this assignment?" I said, feeling uneasy. I pulled the microscope towards me.

"Please, go right ahead," he said. "We need to identify these unmarked specimens. Why don't you start things off? I bet you were some hotshot biology student back in Phoenix. I'm sure this will all be a breeze for you."

How the hell did he know that? He never talked to anyone but his siblings, so it should have been impossible for him to know anything about me. I slowly shook my head in utter bewilderment, then sat up in my chair and straightened my "Phoenix H.S. Remedial Biology 2007 Club Champion" shirt to remove the creases. I was ready to show him how intelligent I was.

"Allow me." Edweird said. He delicately pulled off a thin layer of onion skin and gently placed it on the glass side. He then positioned the slide on the microscope platform directly below the eyepiece. Every movement he made was graceful, like some kind of graceful animal that was moving gracefully. I had to force myself to look away from this impossibly fantastic being and turn my attention to the task at hand. After staring through the eyepiece at the specimen for a long ten seconds, I looked up and gave Edweird a sly smile.

"Onion cells!" I proudly announced.

"Dang, you are one smart girl. And pretty, too. Scientifically speaking, I can safely say that you are pretty smart."

Me, pretty? I hadn't been called "pretty" since I signed up for the *Natural Beauty Cosmetics* pyramid scheme two years ago. And I'd be lying to you if I said my heart wasn't pounding a mile a minute. The sudden rush of blood to my brain made me feel faint, but this time I forced myself to stay conscious.

"Maybe *you* should identify the next slide," I suggested.

"Sounds good to me," Edweird said. He then took an eyedropper and suctioned some cloudy liquid from an unmarked container. He placed a few drops on a clean slide and slid it onto the platform. He then leaned over to my side of the table, nearly brushing up against me as he stared down the eyepiece. I had never been this close to Edweird before. Of course, we only met a few hours ago. I inhaled deeply, taking in his scent. Then my eyes started to water. I have to be honest: The boy had this horrendous gamey smell and was in desperate need of a shower, or at least a stronger deodorant. Regardless, I inexplicably found his odor intoxicating.

"Hmm," he muttered while examining the slide. "This one is extremely…curious."

"What do you mean, Edweird?" I asked.

Edweird lifted his head and looked hard into my eyes. "I believe that this specimen contains some type of miniature tea leaves," he said. "It requires psychic abilities to interpret the different symbols and patterns to find their true meaning. And I'm just the man to do that."

I swallowed hard. "What is it telling you?"

Edweird paused for a long moment. "I'm too embarrassed to say," he said, unable to look into my eyes. "It's best that I don't comment on this."

"That's not fair," I objected. "Don't tease me, and then leave me hanging. You started something here, and you must finish it. Tell me what you see. *Please*."

"Very well," he said, and once again stared down the eyepiece. "I see the entire universe. I see your soul. And I see myself. And baby makes three. Wait, that's not a baby, it's just a very good looking hedgehog. I believe that we are at a small farm or petting zoo. But this is all in the future. And everywhere I look, there you are. This simply cannot be. It makes no sense at all."

I stared at Edweird in disbelief, unable to speak. But Edweird kept staring down the microscope, making slight adjustments to the slide, and never looked up. I thought he was done with his readings, but a moment later he continued his interpretation.

"And if I turn the slide just a tiny bit, I see a black cat in a pink tutu cooking a vegetarian soufflé. Now *that's* odd."

I felt my jaw drop. Unfortunately, some of the fruit flies that had escaped from their container had flown into my mouth. That, combined with Edweird's psychic reading of this mysterious substance (which I later discovered was simply pond scum) had my head whirling once again. What exactly did the future hold for us, and why didn't it make any sense to him?

We finished identifying the remaining substances in complete silence. When the bell rang Edweird was already packed and ready to go. He seemed to be in a hurry to leave. What was he running from?

"See you later, Stella. But probably not," he said, and then quickly flew out of the room.

What did he mean by that? Why was he playing with my mind? All I wanted was a normal first day of school, and half way into it my head was already spinning. This is not a good thing: we Crows do not do well with mystery and confusion. Not well at all. Just look at ol' Harley. Need I say more?

3. SLIP SLIDING AWAY

THE NOVELTY OF BEING at a new school had quickly worn off, and over the next several weeks I fell into a comfortable routine. My classes were rather easy for me, far less challenging than my prior school in Phoenix. I ended up placing out of both my remedial reading and remedial math classes, and was assigned to advanced remedial reading and math classes. Advanced Pig Latin class was a breeze since I grew up speaking that at home. And I regularly copied off of Maria's exams in Spanish class and never got less than a perfect score. So all in all, things were humming along rather smoothly.

Things had also remained somewhat awkward between Edweird and me, but it wasn't like I was obsessing over him. Actually I was. Who am I trying to fool? But since the first day of school he had kept a noticeable distance from me, and I had made no effort to approach him either. Whenever we passed each other in the hall we would both politely smile, but that was pretty much it. Nope, I was not going to be caught up in some weird situation here. That just was not my style.

It was now late October and another wretched school day had come to an end. The weather forecasters had predicted that today, for the third time this calendar year, the sun would actually appear. Immediately after class I ran outside with great anticipation, energized by my fond memories of my time back in Phoenix, where the hot, sunny skies would greet us after the final school bell had sounded. But nay, no sun would shine on this day. The skies were again angry, and cried their displeasure down on us. In no time we were covered in moisture. But this was no ordinary precipitation; it was the kind of really cold rain that, because the temperature had dropped below freezing, seemed to form a frozen substance. Being from Arizona, I knew nothing of this cold, magical powder from the sky that the white man calls "snow." It frightened me.

I carefully walked to the parking lot, surmising that my truck was where I had last left it this morning. About fifty yards away I could see Edweird standing alone next to a gray Volvo, which I had recognized as the vice principal's car. Edweird was holding a long hose and an empty bucket and, as far as I could tell, was surreptitiously siphoning gas out of its gas tank. Although I could barely make out his form, I sensed that he could see me clearly, and was assessing me. I don't know why I felt this way, but my feelings were strong. Then he yelled out, "Hey

Stella! I can see you from here, and I'm assessing you at this very moment!" My instincts were right.

Suddenly, I saw his gaze focus on something directly behind me. In a split second, I knew what it was: The unmistakable sound of a 1975 Ford Pinto, with both rack *and* pinion steering, was haphazardly speeding through the parking lot and heading right towards me. The driver—Peter, the school midget who appropriately was also voted class clown—was frantically trying to control his vehicle, but to no avail. His tiny arms with miniature biceps and stubby fingers could not force the relatively oversized steering wheel to turn. Plus, his head was like three feet below the windshield, so for all we know, this was just another typical drive in the park for "Pint-sized" Pete.

Some people who have stared death straight in the eye and defied its calling, claimed to have seen their lives flash before them. At this particular moment I can say the same thing happened to me. In the blink of an eye, my mind had summoned my entire seventeen years of my life: My parents holding me so close and tight the day I was born, preventing oxygen to the part of my brain that controls major bodily functions; my Broadway tour of *Annie*, where I played the little mutt, Scraps; my first grade visit to the state capital to see William Marshall, the Republican Senator from the great state of Arizona; my first French kiss, also from the Republican Senator from Arizona; my teammates piling on me after I scored the winning goal for the U.S. Hockey team in Lake Placid as we miraculously beat the mighty Russians in the 1980 Olympics. And, of course, all those years I spent in the Phoenix General Hospital mental ward suffering from hallucinations and delusions of grandeur.

I opened my eyes and saw that Pete's car was bearing down on me. I could see lil' Pete standing up on the seat, his miniature head bobbing just above the dashboard, and his beady little eyes—eyes that were as imperfect as Edweird's were perfect—staring at me, apologetically. I had at that moment resigned myself to an untimely death. My only wish was that it would be painless, or better yet, quite enjoyable. Hell, it was my wish, why settle for mediocrity, when you can go out with a bang? No pun intended. Again I closed my eyes. My sense of hearing now took over, eclipsing all of my other senses, except for taste and smell. And touch. And probably pain.

I can't personally attest to what happened next, but I'll share with you what I was later told by those who witnessed the event. As Pete's car was seconds away from striking me, "Lumpy," who I need not tell you is an exceptionally large kid, was passing by me on the way to his 1978 AMC Pacer. Naturally, he was too engrossed in his Taco Bell Supreme burrito and chocolate Yoo-Hoo to notice the unfolding events. I won't bore you with all the gory details, so let me just say that Lumpy—may he rest in peace—ended up being my guardian angel, albeit a really obese one. His massive body took the full brunt of the Pinto's impact, which came to an immediate stop and, of course, instantaneously ignited. Sadly, Lumpy didn't make it; but more importantly, I did, completely un-injured. However, when I stood up to do my little celebratory dance I slipped on the ice, falling and smacking my head hard on the cold pavement. For a moment I was completely knocked out. I opened my eyes a second later and there was Edweird standing over me. Was I dreaming? Was I dead? Was I dreaming that I was dead? Was I dead, yet still dreaming? What else? Or, was I dreaming that I was dead, when in fact, I was really dead, but nonetheless dreaming? Nope, just a slight concussion; but Edweird was next to me. My perfect Edweird.

"Edweird," I said. "How...? What...? You were so far away a moment ago, but now, you're here? I mean, if you sprinted it would have taken you 9.147 seconds to get here. But you got here in 2.044 seconds, easily shattering the world record mark I had set in the 1968 Summer Olympics in Mexico City. I don't understand this. What gives?"

"Whatever do you mean?" Edweird replied, staring down at my lovely face. "I was nearby, just... umm... securing the gas cap from that, uh, Dodge Neon right over there. See? It's only about 20 feet away. I just casually strolled over here, in no time at all—technically, 2.249 seconds. Obviously, that fall you just took made you kind of woozy and now you're talking nonsense, not that you're the sharpest knife in the drawer to begin with. My dear Stella, you just went through a major ordeal. We should get you to the hospital—just hop on my back, and I'll run you over there in no time flat."

"Excuse me?" I said. "Did you say, 'hop on my back'? What the hell are you talking about, Eddie?"

"No!" He quickly protested. I said, "Hop... *in the back*...of my car, and I'll drive you over there in no time."

"Right now my head is spinning and I feel so confused. And that is so unlike me." I said dejectedly.

"I know that, Stella," he said in his silky smooth voice, not unlike John Lovitz after inhaling a helium balloon. "But I really think you need immediate medical attention. Let's get you to a hospital—*stat*!"

Those were the last words I remember hearing. At that moment I blacked out into Edweird's arms. Although he initially dropped me, he was right there to pick me back up. My hero!

4. PAGING DR. SULLEN

"IS SHE...*DEAD*?" asked Dr. Carpile Sullen, visiting surgeon at Sporks Community Medical Hospital. Dr. Sullen had just entered my hospital room, carrying a clipboard and a book of *Mad Libs*.

I sat up from my bed and put down the New York Times bestseller *An Idiots Guide to Vampires and Werewolves.* I looked up at the doctor, feebly forcing a smile on my face.

"I kid, I kid!" He blurted out, laughing so hard that his copy of *Cracked* Magazine flew out of his hand. "Hey, you don't get an honorary medical degree from Sporks Community College Correspondence Medical School and Male Modeling University without developing a sense of humor."

Dr. Sullen then pivoted around to examine himself in the full-length mirror attached to the closet door. He pouted his perfect plump lips, ran his hands through his brown, wavy hair, admiring his perfectly tanned complexion. He adjusted his Speedo under his cotton shorts, and ran his hands up and down his freshly shaven, ultra smooth legs. He smiled and winked at his own reflection. He was looking oh-so-fine and he knew it. What was most puzzling to me, though, was why he was wearing shorts in the winter.

"Hi, Dr. Sullen," I said. "You know, I go to school with a bunch of kids with the last name 'Sullen.' Are you related to them?"

"No, you must have me confused with another Dr. Sullen; I get that all the time," he said. I then saw his face scrunch up dramatically. "Oh, wait. That's right, I did adopt a bunch of kids decades ago—I mean a few years back. Completely slipped my mind. Sure, those kids are mine."

I saw Dr. Sullen's eyes quickly shift from side to side, and a bead of sweat began to roll down his face. He then spotted Harley in the room.

"Harley, Stella is going to be fine," he said to my dad who was slumped in a chair in front of the TV. Harley's attention was completely on Barney the purple dinosaur and his young friends. The group of them had broken into a disgustingly sweet closing song. "I'll give her a half kilo of morphine and PCP—*Columbian Gold*—for the pain. She can shoot herself up any time she feels uncomfortable. But she should be back to herself by tomorrow."

Harley's smile grew even wider. "I love you, doc. And you love me. We're a happy family!" He clapped his hand fervently to emphasize his joy.

Dr. Sullen nodded, then reached for Harley's big glass container of M&Ms, picked out a green one, and popped it in Harley's mouth. "We sure are, Harley. We sure are."

Just then Edweird appeared at the doorway, holding a Drakes Devil Dog and a large bottle of tomato juice he had just stolen from the cafeteria. He opened the bottle and began to chug its contents, not stopping to breathe until the bottle was completely empty. Some of the juice had slipped out and trickled down his face. The deep red sheen now coated his chin. This seemed to give him quite a pick-me-up.

"Damn, I should have had a V8!" Edweird blurted out then cackled loudly. "Heyyyyyy, Mr. C.!" he called to Harley, giving him the double 'thumbs up' sign.

Harley, who was now glued to kids TV show *Dora the Explorer*, gave Edweird a casual wave, then returned to the show, singing loudly and remarkably off-key to the '*I'm the Map!*' song. Harley would often shout out directions to Dora using his hand held GPS. If it appeared that she didn't understand him, Harley would place an emergency call to CBS Studios to offer Dora and her monkey companion a police escort to their daily destination.

"Edweird!" I cried out. "You're still here…with *me*…"

"Yes I am, Stella. You are very observant."

Edweird sat down in a chair next to my bed. He seemed genuinely interested in my well-being, although his body language suggested that he was guarded as well.

I stared hard into Edweird's face. I knew so little about him. But what I did know was that this boy was something special. From my perspective he was the most perfect thing to have ever walked the earth. I only hoped that he was one-tenth as beautiful inside as he was on the outside. (I would later discover that the figure was closer to one-ten-thousandth). I needed to learn more about him, and to clear up some things that just did not make sense to me at all.

"Edweird," I said, "what happened in that parking lot made no sense to me what-so-ever. You ran over to me in world record time, and you didn't even have time to stretch beforehand. So, please explain to me what is going on. I want to know the truth."

For a long moment Edweird considered what I had said. He then reached in his backpack, pulled out a pair of dark plastic glasses with an extremely large nose and mustache, and put it on his face. "You want to know the *tooth*? Why that's the craziest thing I've ever heard!" he said in a rather lame Groucho Marx voice.

"Enough of the disguises, Edweird. I don't want to play games with you. Well, maybe Chutes and Ladders. It's Harley's favorite. But damn it Edweird, you need tell me the truth about you. I think I deserve that."

"The truth? You want the *truth*? You can't *handle* the truth!" Edweird snapped, glowering at me. "What do you think is going on? I'm so interested in your whacked out theories. I so want to hear them. Oh please, do share!"

I was not pleased by his sarcastic tone, but I pressed on.

"You want to know what I think? Well, try this one on for size." I took a deep breath, measuring what I was about to say. "I think you are a freak of nature. I believe that you are some type of space traveler, or some guy from Sweden or south Detroit. I think that secretly you yearn to host your own Cajun cooking show on the Food Network, or head up the local PTA. And I think that deep down you are hurting and as confused as I am. That's what I think."

Edweird turned his head and slowly removed his Groucho Marx glasses. "Is that what you really think, Stella? You have me pinned as some kind of freakazoid? Girl, you have quite the imagination, I must say. I'm sure that nasty bump on your head isn't helping matters either."

"I'm fine!" I insisted. "And no, I don't think that you are a monster. I'm just trying to make sense of it all. This whole thing is freaking *me* out. It's such a freaky scene. I'm a super freak, super freak, I'm super freaky, yeow."

Edweird and I sat in silence for the next few moments. The TV began to malfunction and I could see Harley becoming a bit annoyed. Physically I was feeling fine; perhaps all the drugs that Dr. Sullen had pumped into my system were masking the pain. Regardless, I didn't see the need to spend any more time in a hospital room.

An hour later I was officially discharged from the hospital. I said my goodbyes to Dr. Sullen, but Edweird could barely make eye contact with me. Harley then drove us home in his police car. When we arrived at the house Harley ran inside and got himself some milk and cookies, then went right to bed. I, however, was much too wired to sleep: My head was still spinning from everything that had happened in the last twenty-four hours and from the Columbia Gold. Rather than staring at the darkness, I decided it was time to write a letter to my mother.

My mother was my best friend in the whole world. Before she kicked me out of the house, not a day went by when we didn't spend hours talking about our lives, our dreams, and circus snack food. But now we were a thousand miles apart. My sudden relocation made me think that not too long ago people could only stay in touch by writing letters, which was painfully slow, or with expensive long distance phone calls. Today, well, we have everything from emails, to text messages, to cell phones, and internet blogs that could keep us in touch instantly, no matter how far apart we were. There is every opportunity keep in touch with your loved ones if you really wanted to. I figured I'd reach out to mom maybe twice a year, if I got around to it. I decided to get my first letter out of the way.

Dear Mom,

How's it going? Things here suck. The sun never shines and Harley's house smells like a wet dog. School stinks pretty bad, too, but at least no one seems to hate me as much as they did back home. I guess they just don't know me yet.

The one good thing so far is that Harley got me a truck. It's old, ugly, and unreliable. I always think of Harley every time I start her up.

That's all that's going on with me. I hope to see you soon, certainly no later than when book number two comes out, published by the fine people at Little, Brown and Company, and read to you on audio-books by Ilyana Kadushin.

P.S. Did I ever thank you for kicking me out of the house? If not, let me just extend a giant "thanks a lot, mom!" to you right here and now.

Send money!

Luv,

Stella

I folded the letter and stuffed it into an envelope. I decided to give her a wonderful surprise and send it directly to her work. I didn't know the actual address so I simply wrote on the envelope "Stella's Mom aka Gargantuan Sideshow Lady, Phoenix Circus, AZ." Hey, if a letter addressed to "Santa Clause, North Pole" can reach its destination, then why can't mine?

I suddenly felt extremely tired and kind of dopey. A moment later, I drifted off into a dreamless sleep. Or maybe I just dreamed that I did. Who the hell knows?

5. LA SHOVE

I RETURNED TO SCHOOL the next day and was greeted by a bunch of students who were anxious to hear first-hand what had happened to me in the parking lot. They clung to every word I said, and we took time to say a little prayer for poor Lumpy. May his three hundred pound soul rest in peace. After I told my story—skipping the part about Edweird flying over to me, of course—the students dispersed and went about their business. My friends Maria and Erik stayed behind until they were convinced that I was perfectly fine. They also informed me that a bunch of kids were heading out this weekend to a small town called La Shove, which is widely known for its spectacular beaches. Maria insisted that I make plans to go.

"Sure, I'll go. I need to get away for a while," I told them.

"It's settled then." Maria said. "We'll pick you up Saturday afternoon and the three of us will drive there together."

The rest of the week went by rather quickly. I didn't run into Edweird or any of the Sullens, and no one seemed to know where they disappeared to. I must say that his absence gave me a mental vacation I so needed. Tending to my school work and raising Harley was a full time job in itself; I didn't have time for a boy who was always messing with my head...Ah, who am I kidding? I loved the attention. God, how I missed his cute little butt.

Before I knew it Saturday had arrived. True to their word, Maria and Erik came to my house to pick me up. After a thirty minute drive we arrived at La Shove. And let me just say this: I've never been to Chechnya, Bosnia or Yemen. But if I had, I'm sure I would have felt much more at ease than I did here. The place was an environmental war zone. The toxic waste spewing from the chemical factories turned the ocean a fluorescent green. The smoke from the nuclear power plants turned the sky an eerie grayish hue, and the seagulls were showering uric acid down on us like they had been feasting on Ex-lax. Nonetheless, the kids all seemed to be having a good time—except for the ones who were experiencing toxic shock syndrome. They didn't look happy at all.

From the parking lot I could see in the distance a campsite where most of the kids had gathered. I was too far away to identify any faces, but I figured I'd start walking in that direction nonetheless. I made it to the campsite in fifteen minutes, having fallen no less than a dozen times. My hands were bloodied, but the scar tissue from all my previous falls had killed the nerve endings, so the pain was tolerable. My history of self-inflicted wounds was finally starting to pay dividends.

When I arrived at the campsite I found a beach chair and sat down to rest. Sitting across from me was a small boy with long black hair pulled back in a ponytail. I figured him to be a couple years younger than me, so that would make him…let's see, carry the two…about four…no, make that fifteen. He was very attractive, in a boyish kind of way. His features were like a poor-man's Edweird—an *extremely* poor man—and more roundish. His skin was nearly flawless, save for what appeared to be a *hot spot* on the left side of his face, which looked remarkably similar to the one on our neighbor's collie. I found that a bit peculiar. Anyway, the boy caught me looking his way, then stood up and walked over to me.

"Hi, I'm Yakob Brown." He said, extending his short, hairy arm toward me. "You must be Stella Crow, right?"

"Yes, that's me." I said shaking his hand. "I already know who you are, Yakob. Actually I don't since we've never met. Harley has told me all about you. To be perfectly honest he's said very little. Either way, it's nice to meet you. And for now on you can call me 'Isabella.'"

"Nice to meet you, Stella," he said and then he yipped.

That was strange.

"You know that truck of yours—'Ol' Lemon'—that used to be mine," Yakob said. "My dad was close to torching that suicide machine and driving it off the side of a cliff. But your dad wanted to buy it, so my pop gave it to him for just a few grand, with low, low financing. I guess you must have swiped it from your old man."

"Actually, he gave it to me as a welcome home gift." I said. "He wanted to make my move to Sporks as smooth as possible, and this was his way of doing it."

"Harley's a moron, but he has a heart of gold," Yakob boldly said. "Of course, I'm not telling you anything you don't already know."

"I agree, and no, you're not."

"I'm a bit surprised Ol' Lemon is still running, to be perfectly honest," Yakob said. "Have you passed out behind the wheel from the carbon monoxide fumes spewing from the air vents? Has the clutch given out, or have the brakes failed? Have you repaired the rusted out holes in the radiator? How about the leaky gas tank, constant oil drip, misaligned front and back wheels, damaged struts, improperly rebuilt engine, or the busted speedometer? Those things holding up?"

"So far so good," I said, feeling both impressed and horrified by his honesty and boyish innocence. "I even managed to make the car's interior look respectable once I vacuumed up all the dog hair. How many dogs do you have?"

He looked at me quizzically, not saying anything, scratched his ear with his left hand and then licked the back of it.

I immediately trusted Yakob. He seemed so warm and genuine, even though he was short and past the age where a growth spurt was likely. A wise man once said, "Short people got no reason to live." But this boy was different. We ended up talking for the next couple of hours, and even when I said something he didn't agree with, he rarely *glowered* at me. I'm the kind of girl who doesn't like to be glowered at. Call me old fashioned, but glowering is just not my cup of tea.

"So," Yakob said to me later that evening, "I hear you've got the *hots* for one of the Sullen boys. Edweird, is it? Boy, do I have some stories to tell about them. You just wouldn't believe the rumors. Unbelievable. Absolutely mind-boggling. Amazing. Earth-shattering. Mind blowing, knock your socks off. Bowl you over. Completely life changing. But, you probably aren't interested, so never mind."

Needless to say I was a tad interested. I trust that this doesn't come as a surprise to you. Of course, I noticed that none of the Sullens were at this party, and I had wanted to ask Yakob why not.

"Why not?" I asked, inquiring as to why none of the Sullens were at the party.

"The Sullens don't come to these parties, or any other social gatherings for that matter," Yakob said, as he turned to howl at the moon. His actions caught me off guard, and I gave out a nervous laugh. He quickly twisted his head towards me, glowering.

"Not everyone is fond of the Sullens. Don't trust whitey," he said. His innocent eyes looked into my dark, jeweled peepers. "Let's stroll along the beach. If you'd like, I can tell you some stories about the people who live in these parts. We can start with my family."

"Um, yeah, sure, I guess." I said smoothly, like a singing nightingale.

Yakob and I began walking along the beach, our bare feet leaving footprints in the cool sand. Tiny shards of glass were embedding in my heels with every step I took. Farther down the shore scores of beached whales blocked our path, providing us an opportunity to utilize our athleticism. Yakob hoisted himself on the largest whale we found, then extended his hand down to me to pull me up. He was remarkably weak, even for his slight size, and I ultimately lifted myself on the enormous beast. Once on top of the rotting animal the view looking out over the ocean was, as described, spectacular. The toxic spills had created a potpourri of colors not normally found in nature. And for the first time I was truly glad that I lived here. Although it was a quiet town and nothing exciting ever happened, I found harmony and inner peace being completely surrounded by chemicals and materials not found anywhere else. And it gave me great comfort knowing that if I had to pass gas, the horrendous smells of the rotting carcasses and the chemical stench emanating from the crashing waves would cover my noxious fumes with nary a backward glance.

"So, I'm still confused about the Sullens," I said. "Why don't they come here? Aren't they invited?"

Yakob looked out over the ocean, then tilted his head toward the sky. He seemed to fixate on the second star to the right, and straight on 'til morning. Then he looked down to his tiny feet, and then at my normal size feet, and lifted his eyes up to my calves, knee caps, hips, thighs, and buttocks, my incredible knockers if I do say so myself, chin and eventually, my eyes.

"I'm sorry, were you talking to me?" he asked innocently. "I was just thinking about an episode of *The Dog Whisperer* I saw the other day. Did you say something about the Sullens?"

I glowered at him. "Yes," I said, in response to his question.

He paused for a moment, and then he said, "Do you like scary stories?"

"Do I!" I said, not particularly happy that he had apparently changed subjects, but delighted at the prospect of hearing another ghost story. Maybe it was one I had never heard before. I always loved hearing the story of where the babysitter is receiving those awful phone calls, which are coming from inside the house!

"Well, this scary story has to do with the Sullens." He said. "Come, let's have a seat on this pile of this algae-laden/chemical oozing drift wood."

We both slid down the whale and Yakob walked up to the pile of soaking wood, circled around it twice, sniffed into the wind, then gently seated himself. I squatted a few feet away.

"Before I tell you stories about the Sullens, let me start by first telling you about my family, the Quailettes," he said. "This won't take long—thirty, forty-five minutes tops, without any commercial interruptions."

"Oh, what joy," I said. "Please begin, I haven't got all day."

"Very well." Yakob said, pulling an engorged tick off his arm. "Some say that thousands of years ago

Quailettes descended from fish—you know, guppies, angel fish, perch, and tuna helper. We evolved at phenomenal rates, both physically and intellectually. Emotionally, well, we're still somewhere between a striped bass and a piranha. Over time, we evolved into birds, then dog-like creatures, back to birds, then a herring, then a superhuman being, then took a giant step back and became a domesticated ferret, before arriving at what we are today. The elders believe that our next transformation will either be some type of insect or an English Bull Dog named Trixie. Although there is absolutely no scientific proof whatsoever that such an evolution took place, I personally believe the theory is pretty air tight. Either way, it makes for a good story to tell at beach parties. Chicks seem to dig it."

I nodded politely, hoping that I didn't just waste three minutes of my life I'll never get back.

"But there are some who disagree with how the Quailettes came to be," Yakob continued. "Some elders tell stories of how our ancestors lived among the wolves in the majestic mountains near the Indies, known to its inhabitants as 'The Mountains Near the Indies.' Though not friends, the wolves and my human ancestors lived as peaceful neighbors, often borrowing cups of sugar from each other when food supplies were scarce, or if the grocery stores were closed. The wolves and the humans had no reason to fear each other, or any other creatures in the living in the area.

As you know, wherever there is life, there are spirits living close by. Sadly, the spirits who lived in the Indies were mostly evil. From time to time, these evil spirits would threaten the lives of all living creatures in that region. Sometimes the spirits attacked the wolves, and sometimes they attacked the humans. But each pack fought bravely and defeated the evil spirits.

One dark winter's night, the most evil spirit of all, known as Behn Affleckian, had entered The Mountains Near The Indies, looking to rid the land of all humans and wolves. Without warning, the evil spirit Affleckian attacked each pack, hoping to first divide, and then ultimately destroy, both of them. Neither pack alone could defeat this evilest of all spirits. However, working together, man and wolf would forge a more powerful bond to fight off this spirit enemy. Fighting together and standing as one, man and wolf created a positive life force energy field that no evil spirit could penetrate. The two packs had defeated the Behn Affleckian spirit and made The Mountains Near the Indies safe from his presence and his feature movies forever.

Later that night was the scene of an unprecedented victory celebration, the likes that had not been seen for a long, long time in a place far, far away, when man and Ewok rejoiced after defeating the Evil Empire. The Mountains Near the Indies became the site of a Roman-like orgy. With spirits—this time, *alcoholic* ones—flowing freely (the wolves had managed to purchase a keg from the 24-hour drive through liquor store) the festivities had gone too far. The humans and wolves first swapped stories of their victories, but after several shots of tequila with Bud Lite chasers, also swapped mates. Pretty much everyone was doing the nasty with anything with a heartbeat. From this night on, the future generations of wolves and humans would forever be linked.

And that brings me to my line of ancestors: My great, great grandfather, "Screaming Wolf Biyatch" and his son "How Much Did You Drink, Dad?" and his son, "Grandpa Did What, and With Whom?" and his son, "You're Shittin' Me!" and of course my father, "Billy." So I was given the name "Yakob" which loosely translates to "Great, Great Grandchild of man who allegedly had sex with a large, hairy dog."

I remained silent for a while, trying to digest this extraordinary tale. "Um, that's just swell. That's, really...*something*. Super duper. So...what about the Sullens? You said you'd tell me about them."

Yakob seemed a little disappointed that I had not shown one iota of interest in his tales of bravery, survival, and bestiality. Quite honestly, if I were him, I'd stick to the fish story, and end it there. But, I'd figure I'd sit patiently as he blah, blah, blahed his whole family tree so I could get him to tell me tales of who I was most interested in—The Sullens.

Yakob sat up, quickly scratched himself behind the ear, repeatedly licked his hairy forearms, and then looked up at me. "As you wish. But I'd like to change the pace a little. You know, my throat is sore from talking so much. So, what would you think if I tell you about the Sullens through interpretive dance? Honestly, I'm quite good at it, and I usually charge admission, or at the very least ask for a box of treats. But for you, tonight's performance it's on the house."

I stared at him for a moment waiting for the silence to be broken by Yakob uproarious laughter signaling that it was all a joke. It didn't happen. So I nodded my head slowly. "I kind of would like to hear the story through spoken word. But, if you must dance, then dance you will. Dance to the music. Dance the night away. Dance, dance, dance. Dance, as if no one is watching. Everybody's dancing in the moonlight. You are the Dancing Queen, young and sweet, only seventeen. Come on baby, do the locomotion."

Yakob nodded back at me. He then walked over to a tree stump, hoisted himself up, and struck a pose, as if he were an Olympic ice skater waiting for the music to kick off their routine. A moment later he pirouetted a full circle, jumped twice clicking his heals, and did some type of shuffle with his arms extended and rotating counter clockwise. Then, he got on his hands and knees and began barking like a slightly injured dog, before turning on his back and spinning himself for a good thirty seconds. As he slowed, his arms and legs each spun in opposite directions, not unlike a chicken that had been shot through cannon. When his spinning stopped, he stood up on his toes, closed his eyes, and yelped three times. He then dismounted the tree stump and looked intently to my face, waiting for my reaction.

I quickly stood up and looked hard into Yakob's eyes. "Jimmy's fallen into a well? And the Sullens are...are...*vampires*?"

"Easy girl, easy now!" He said. "Jimmy will be fine; the fire department will see to that. And the Sullens, well, we're not exactly one hundred percent sure about them. Closer to ninety-eight point six. But riddle me this: What's cold, about a hundred years old, and are also known as 'blood suckers'?"

"Hmmm, I'm not sure. My Great Uncle Louis?"

"No, I'm afraid that's not right. The answer we were looking for is "vampires." We would have also accepted "The Sullens." I'm so sorry. But thank you for playing, you've been a delightful contestant, and we have some lovely parting gifts for you."

So the Sullens were vampires, or at least that's the word on the street. I couldn't wait to see Edweird. He sure had a lot of 'splainin' to do.

6. THE DREAM

I THOUGHT ABOUT EVERYTHING that Yakob had said (or danced) during the drive home that night. He wasn't just dancing out a fancy folk tale; he truly believed the stories of the werewolves and the vampires. When I got home I found Harley glued to the TV, eating a bowl of Cheese Doodles and flipping channels back and forth between "Hawaii Five-0" and "Hannah Montana." My God he's an idiot.

"Hi, Harley," I said as I walked into the house. "I'm pretty tired. I think I'll just head on up to my room, if that's okay."

Harley had a perplexed look on his face, and never took his eyes off the TV screen. "What the hell? By day she's a student, and at night she this international pop star? And no one even knows! Is that even *possible*? Someone's bound to find out. I mean, give me a break!"

"It's a mystery to me too, Pops," I replied, tired and disinterested. "Good luck figuring this one out."

"Book him, Dano!" He blurted out while wildly clapping his hands. He had a very satisfied look on his face.

"Well done, dad. Another case solved."

"Sweet dreams, Stella," he said, playing with his toes.

I walked up to my room and immediately flung myself onto the bed. I grabbed my CD player, put my headphones on, and immediately started to drift off. I opened my eyes and found myself standing on a beach, one that I had never seen before. I started walking along the shore, but didn't see anyone for miles. I was surrounded by crashing waves, a cloudless sky, and a slightly cool breeze. I continued to walk and walk and walk, mile after mile after mile. I sat on a bench to rest for a while, then walked some more. And still nothing. The sun was beginning to set, and my legs were getting tired. And then I woke up.

"That dream sucked." I thought to myself. "Let's see if I can do any better next time."

Once again I drifted off quickly, and began to dream. This time I found myself in an open field surrounded by thick woods. On the far side of the field were two dozen penguins playing a modified game of rugby while dressed in fluorescent-colored French bikinis and carrying 16-pound bowling balls. One penguin would roll the ball at another unsuspecting one, knocking him into the goal, and setting off a chorus of cheers from a group of Pygmies and giant lizards covered in chocolate.

"Stella!" A voiced called from behind me. "I found you, thank God."

It was Mike, a kid I knew from school.

"Mike, what's wrong?" I said.

Mike ran up next to me, trying to catch his breath. "You need to leave this place. It's not safe," he said urgently.

"I don't want to leave, Mike. I've got fifty bucks on the Seattle Penguins, and they need my support."

"Trust me, Stella. This is not a place you want to be…Oh no, what's that?"

Suddenly, we heard shuffling coming from the forest. We stared in the general direction of the sound until two figures appeared. A moment later I recognized the first one to be Edweird, and right next to him was Yakob. They were holding hands as they headed toward Mike and me. I thought I saw Yakob give Edweird a slight peck on the cheek.

"I'm outta here," Mike said, then grabbed a unicycle from his shirt pocket and rode away while juggling six coconuts and singing an old Celtic love song. A few seconds later the two boys were standing next to me.

"Edweird? Yakob? What's going on? Why are the two of you together?"

"Stella, it's time that you know. We are lovers," Edweird said, gesturing to Yakob. "Our love dates back almost fifty years. It is a bond that cannot be broken. Many have tried, all have failed. And those who have gotten in our way have paid the ultimate price. It's time for you to get out of our way, Stella, if you know what's good for you."

"But I love YOU, Edweird. Sure, I'll probably hook up with Yakob in *Eclipse*. After all, you're going to leave me for roughly three hundred pages. But that's neither here nor there. You and I were meant to be together. I mean you, me and sometimes Yakob...and sometimes just Yakob and me, but mostly you and me. That's just the way I always dreamed it should be, you want to marry me. We'll marry."

"Hmmm," said Edweird thoughtfully after a long pause. "You know, I'm actually getting kind of tired of Yakob, if you want to know the truth. I mean, seriously, going steady with the same guy for half a century can make for a stale relationship. Maybe it's time we see other people. You really set me straight on this, Stella. I want to thank you for making me see this whole vampire-werewolf relationship thing more clearly."

Edweird then turned to Yakob, who had remained silent throughout. "It's over between us, toots."

Edweird reached out his tattooed arm and softly patted Yakob's head. He then tightly gripped his fingers around Yakob's noggin, and spun it around like a top. After about a dozen or so rotations Yakob's head popped off, and Edweird casually flung it into the Penguins' goal, tying the score and forcing the game into overtime. Again, the Pygmies and chocolate covered lizards erupted enthuseastically.

Edweird then turned to me, smiling coyly. "Here's looking at you, kid."

I abruptly woke up. I had this sudden and unmistakable craving for a hot fudge sundae.

7. PORT ORLEANS

HALLOWEEN WAS FAST APPROACHING and Prozac High School's annual "Blood, Guts and Tears" dance was only a week away. I still hadn't decided if I would be going. No one had asked me to the dance, so if I did go, I'd be going stag. But my two friends, Maria and Jennifer, already had dates and wanted to buy some fancy costumes. The stores in Sporks mostly sold the cheap plastic Halloween outfits for little kids. Anything worth buying would require a trip to the big city, Port Orleans.

I told Harley about my plans to drive to Port Orleans with my two friends. After explaining to him the ritual of Halloween he agreed to let me go. My truck had little chance of making it to the city without breaking down so Jennifer decided to drive the three of us in her car.

We left for Port Orleans right after lunch on Saturday. After getting lost several times, we finally arrived at the Port Orleans outlet center several hours later. The stores were bustling with Halloween shoppers who had also traveled quite a distance to find some great deals. Maria and Jennifer could barely contain themselves when they passed by the first costume store. I, on the other hand, was mostly window shopping. I had already decided that if I were to go to the dance, I could borrow dad's Barney the Dinosaur costume he'd liked to wear to formal police functions or when his drinking buddies came over for a few no holds barred game of Candy Land.

For the next few hours, Maria and Jennifer tried on just about every costume they could get their hands on. Although they seemed to be enjoying themselves, I was getting pretty bored. They were also talking incessantly about their dates to the dance—how dreamy they were, and how they were nearly perfect in every way. Sheesh. I cannot begin to tell you how annoying that was. I mean, can you imagine page after page going on and on about how hot and perfect someone was, ad nauseum? It was enough to make me tear my hair out. So I glowered at them.

They were also surprised when I told them that no one had asked me to the dance. Jennifer mentioned that she'd be willing to set me up with a rather plain but very friendly girl in her auto shop class who would be perfect for me. When I told them I'd rather go with a boy, they had a perplexed look on their faces. They scoffed when I told them that just because I don't *date* boys doesn't mean that I prefer to be with girls. But the fact that I didn't have a date at all was suddenly bringing me down.

After this rather depressing conversation, I decided that I needed some time alone. So I left the store and started walking down the street, trying to clear my head. I took a shot of whisky from the emergency flask I had secretly hidden in my purse. I quickly felt my insides beginning to warm up. My brain also began to take notice and started to tingle.

During my time alone, I had inadvertently wandered down some unfamiliar streets and no longer recognized my surroundings. It was early evening and the streets were busy with commuters. However, in my tipsy stupor, I had unknowingly turned down a few alleyways, climbed up some fire escapes, slid down a garbage chute, and took a catnap inside an old metal dumpster. When I came to my senses, it was *twilight* (wink, wink, nod, nod). The evening calm was suddenly interrupted by the sounds of rowdy banter and laughter headed my way. Four men were casually wandering the streets, and when they spotted me, they became quiet. I glanced over at them, and then quickly looked away. I could feel their steely gazes upon me. Could almost hear their fractured breathing, and smell the caged desire emanating from them. I became uneasy about this situation—I have a keen sense about these things.

I began walking down the alley in the opposite direction from the men. I quickened my pace, stumbling a few times, but valiantly continued on. I was completely lost, but figured that eventually I would wander to a main road filled with people. After a few minutes, I again heard the same voices of the men I had tried to escape. I had unfortunately circled around the block, and actually ended up closer to them than I had been before. Again, we glanced at each other across the street, staring quietly. The silence was broken by one of the men. I never got his name, so I'll simply call him "Man Number One."

"Hey, pretty girl," he called out to me. I figured he wasn't talking to one of his friends, who were neither attractive nor female. That left me as his addressee. "What's a pretty thing like you doing out here by yourself? You must be looking for a party. Well, the party has arrived. It's your lucky day!"

"Ooooh, I love parties!" I replied. "Birthdays, anniversaries, orgies, Tupperware. It's all real, it's all good. What's the occasion? You know, I could make us some terrific appetizers: bruschetta with goat cheese and fresh tomatoes right off the vine. For the main course, perhaps some roasted chicken with a honey glaze, candied carrots and a Caesar salad. Oh, and for dessert, something light. Hmmm, how about some sorbet and perhaps a light fruit salad? Maybe one of you could pick up some cookies. It doesn't have to be from a bakery, but something nice, like Entenmann's."

I almost instantly regretted sounding too anxious. These preparations would take hours, and I hadn't even gone shopping yet. Besides, it had just occurred to me, I didn't even know these men. I knew nothing about their respective occupations, their hobbies, interests, ambitions, dreams, likes and dislikes. Did they have families? Were they financially secure? Any short term or chronic health concerns? Republican, Democrat, or Independent? Come to think of it, I truly knew nothing about them at all. Curiously, though, they knew nothing about me either, but nonetheless took the initiative to get to know me better. I admired them for that, I truly did.

"No need to bother with all that," said Man Number One. "The party's about to get started, now that you're here. That's all we need."

Then a second man, who I'll refer to as "Man Number Two" joined in. "Yeah, what he said," he said, gesturing to Man Number One.

"Well, I, um…I'm just not sure about this." I explained. "My friends are waiting for me, just a couple blocks away. They both are female, very attractive and weak, pretty defenseless actually, not unlike myself. I could call them on my cell phone and get them over here before you can say "jackpot!"

"That won't be necessary, pretty girl," said Man Number One. "As long as you're here, we got us a fine party on our own."

I was flattered. Apparently, they sensed that I was an excellent conversationalist, an accomplished chef, and could hold my own even in an unfamiliar setting. But, again, I sensed that they were withholding some key information about this party from me—information that would be important in deciding whether to stay or leave.

"Fellas, you are all so sweet. I'd love to stay and get to know you all intimately. But it's getting late, so let's just take a rain check. How about I get your phone numbers, and we can make plans to meet up again? Sound good?"

The four men looked at one another incredulously. I had made a pretty convincing argument, I thought, and guessed they were nonverbally debating its merits with one another. They smiled at each other then began laughing heartily. I instantly felt a great sense of relief. Nothing bad could happen when four horny, drunken men were together laughing. Hey, I might live in a small town *now*, but I grew up in the big city. I was worldly, I knew stuff. I could handle myself perfectly well, thank you very much.

"Well then, it's settled." I said. "We'll plan on having a party next week. You guys are great. I feel so close to each one of you. I really think we have something special going on here. So, let's keep in touch, and you boys stay out of trouble."

The men stared at each other, again in disbelief. They laughed even harder this time, but not the kind of laugh of the joyful and innocent. This laugh had an edge to it, a sharp edge—the kind of sharp edge that, if rusty, would give you tetanus if you hadn't been inoculated in the last ten years. No, this was not a welcoming laugh. It was the opposite kind. It was an *un*welcoming laugh. My spider senses were tingling again.

I quickly turned around, and began walking away from them. I was in full stride when I heard their footsteps coming from behind me. I started to walk serpentine, in an effort to lose them. Unfortunately, I had not practiced this maneuver in quite some time, and twice stumbled during the sharp cutback, cutting my knees pretty badly. Again, I heard laughter from behind. I quickened my pace, walking in a straight line to prevent further self-inflicted injuries. This strategy seemed to work. I only fell once, and began to distance myself from these men. I looked back quickly, and saw only Man Number One and the second man—Man Number Two—looking at me from a block away.

I turned the corner hoping to see a major street. No such luck, just another dark, vacant road. I had no choice but to continue walking. I no longer heard footsteps from behind me. I began to feel better about things. Sure, I had never gotten their phone numbers to call them about our party next week. But in reality, I was not in the mood. A minute or two later I was at the end of the street, and had another decision to make. Left, right, or straight? Before I could decide, however, I saw two figures slowly making their way towards me. As they reached the street light, I recognized them as the other two men in the group. They smiled, but not welcoming. The third man, who I had mistakenly labeled "Man Number Four," started to speak.

"Pretty girl, what's your hurry? Are you trying to run away from us? You know, that's quite rude of you. We were just trying to be nice to you, and this is the thanks we get. I think it's time we teach you a little lesson about common courtesy."

The fourth man, who I now had no choice but to refer to as "Man Number Three," interjected: "Yeah, what he said."

My heart was now beating a million miles a second. I was starting to feel the adrenaline pumping through my blood. I felt my muscles tense up. Fight or flight. I knew I couldn't outrun them all, so fighting was my only option. If it came to that, I was going to go down swinging. I knew I couldn't win, but I wanted to go the distance. Maybe even get a draw. But a unanimous decision just didn't seem to be in the cards. Now, it was a matter of deciding how I would engage them: Nails? Teeth? Pulling hair? Knee to the groin? One from column A, two from column B? Or perhaps some form of martial arts, but which kind? Judo? Karate? Kung Fu? Then more decisions: Tiger, crane, cobra? Wax on, or wax off? So many decisions, so little time. All I knew was this: No mercy. Mercy was for the weak. Sweep the leg, finish them. Do you have a problem with that? No sensei!

"Get away from me...I'm warning you!" I managed to stammer out. By now, the other two men had caught up to me, and the four started to position themselves around me.

"Ooh, you're a feisty one. I like that," Man Number Four said. "A little spunk, and a lot of chutzpah. You got style, lady. There's an old Pig Latin saying for what you have, and it goes something like this..."

Just then, a car came flying around the corner, nearly hitting a stray cat that had wandered on to the street. The car stopped right in front of us, and the driver's side window opened. The driver leaned over to me, looked me straight into my eyes, and asked, "Would you like to buy some Girl Scout cookies? My daughter needs to sell three more boxes, and she'll win an all expense paid trip to Seattle next summer. Five bucks a box, two for ten. It's a great deal, buy now and save. How many can I put you down for?"

I was caught off guard by this mysterious man, and his generous offer. But my body froze, not knowing what to do or say. Maybe I should jump in his car, explain to him my dire situation, and later decide if I should purchase the Peanut Butter Sandwich/Do-si-dos™ or Thin Mints, and how many. But that might put us both in danger. The driver, unfortunately, was not tolerant of my indecisiveness, and opted to leave before I could make up my mind. He rolled up his window, gave me a disappointed look and quickly sped away. However, just as this car departed, a second one sped around the corner. This driver did manage to run over the stray cat ending its miserable existence. The passenger side door flew open and the driver leaned over, his eyes piercing mine.

"Need a ride, pretty girl?"

"*Edweird*?" I cried out. "Sure, I'd love one! But can I first say goodbye to my friends?" I looked at the four men with mixed feelings then looked back at Edweird. "Ah, what the heck, let's just go."

I jumped in his car and buckled myself in, inserting the metal piece into the other, and adjusting the strap to fit me securely. I also made the decision that if oxygen masks were deployed, I would place the elastic band around my head and pull securely to ensure a proper fit. Then I would ensure that my mask is securely fastened *before* trying to assist other passengers, including small children. This might have seemed a bit selfish, but I believed it was the right thing to do—for both Edweird and me, and for our unborn child. Oops, I'm getting a bit ahead of myself.

As Edweird drove away he glanced quickly at me, his dark eyes piercing my very soul. I noticed that his expression was one of both concern and anger.

"You know, I'm both concerned and angry right now," he said. Boy, I really nailed that one.

I studied his perfect face, his strong jaw and single chin, high cheek bones and full, pouty lips. I felt safe with him, but I also felt that somehow I had let him down.

"Edweird, I made an awful mistake," I said, my eyes beginning to tear up. "I put myself in great danger and could have been seriously injured or maimed. And not only that…because of my stupidity, I might not get ANY Thin Mints or those irresistible Do-si-dos™." I struggled to hold back the fountain of tears I felt forming in my eye ducts.

Edweird studied my lovely face. "I should smack you on the head with a baseball bat for your stupidity," he said. Edweird immediately reached behind him to the back seat of the car and a second later he was holding a Rawlings wooden baseball bat. He waived it frantically around his head, the exact same way the great Willie Mayes used to do during his rookie year, when he hit a solid .291 with 30 home runs for the San Francisco Giants, easily capturing the NL Rookie of the Year award.

There was something about Edweird that I could not explain. He gave me strength. He made me feel safe. When he was around I knew that things would work out, no matter how dire they appeared to be. And when he wasn't around I still got the sense that he was looking after me. He was a part of me, and I truly believed that I was becoming a part of him. He reminded me of Obi Wan Kenobi, but with a wooden baseball bat rather than a light saber. Edweird was my Force—a Force that would always be with me.

Edweird leaned toward me and looked into my eyes. "You know, next to lovin' I like fighting. And since you and I won't be doing any lovin' tonight, we might as well go back and beat the snot out of those four men—Man Number One, Man Number Three, Man Number Four, and Man Number Two, in no particular order. You ready to bust some chops?"

"You know, Edweird" I said, "I think I've had enough excitement for one night. Can't we just go home?"

Just then my stomach growled, but not the kind of growl that a wild animal would make when he is threatened. This was the kind of growl one's stomach makes when that person is either hungry or has minor indigestion. I decided we needed to take a detour to get some food.

"Edweird, wait, I've changed my mind. I'm starving. How 'bout you buy me a steak dinner with your choice of vegetables and all the free refills of soda you can drink. Sorry, no refills after leaving the restaurant. A great deal at $12.99. Tax not included. Your mileage may vary. Offer not valid in California or New Jersey."

"That's a great idea," said Edweird. "Let's go Dutch."

8. MY DINNER WITH EDWEIRD

EDWEIRD AND I DROVE a few more miles down the main road when we came across a small all-night diner. Just what I was looking for. At my urging, Edweird reluctantly pulled into the parking lot and parked near the front door. We walked in the restaurant and were immediately seated at a small table. Perhaps it was my imagination, but it seemed to me like the hostess gave Edweird an extra long look.

"Is this place okay with you?" I asked Edweird, who appeared a little restless.

"Sure, it's fine. Actually, I've been here lots of times. The food is pretty good—so I've been told—and you can't beat the service."

"You've come here before, but never ordered anything to eat?" I asked.

"I don't really eat…that much. It's, uh, kind of a long story. I'd rather not get into right now. Or ever." Edweird replied without sounding defensive.

"Makes no difference to me," I replied. "I'll let you know how the food is."

Just then our waitress arrived at our table, handed each of us a menu, and offered to take our drink order.

"The lady will have a coke, and I'll have the usual, Tammy," Edweird said to our waitress, whose name tag indicated that her name was Mabel.

Mabel first gave me an obligatory smile then turned her attention toward Edweird.

"Hiya, big boy. What's a tall, pale, handsome stud like you doing in a place like this?"

Edweird cackled like a disgustingly obese school girl who was just asked to the prom by a slightly less fat boy. "Oh, Tammy, you're too much."

"It's Mabel. Don't you remember me, Big Ed?"

Edweird stared at her intently, then his eyes widened. "Ummm…no…I don't think we've ever met before. In fact, I'm nearly 100% certain that I've never seen you beyond these walls, especially not during a completely out of control bachelor party at the "Kitty Cat Club" last month. Never happened. No sir, no siree."

"Sure, Big Eddie, whatever you say," she said, rolling her right eye and winking at him with her left. "I just hope you got that little problem of yours taken care of. Hey, it happens to everyone, don't you worry about it one tiny bit."

"Ah, Tammy," Edweird said. "You're such a dirty girl…I mean, *kidder*. You are such a dirty little kidder! I mean, I'm *guessing* that you're a dirty kidder. I don't know you at all, remember?"

I was not entirely sure what the heck was going on here, but the one thing I was absolutely certain about was that Edweird had never met our waitress before. I pretty much figured it was just a matter of mistaken identity. I had a good sense for these things. I had inherited my dad's police detective instincts.

"I'm really hungry. Do you think we can order now?" I asked.

"Sure thing." Edweird said. "Go ahead and order. You can have anything you want tonight, anything at all. Go on, live it up. Price is of no concern to me. None whatsoever. Did I mention I left my wallet at home?"

I scanned the menu and give Mable my order. "Let's see…how about the tiny mushrooms stuffed with lobster, bacon, spam, and caviar. With extra cheese. And would you 'super-size' that?"

"Yeah, sure thing pretty girl, I can do that." Mabel said, unable to hide her disinterest in me.

"Tammy, give me a Vodka straight up, with a bourbon and whiskey chaser. And tack on your finest imported beer to wash it all down." Edweird said.

"Edweird, your soul is so pure, and your mind is always so focused. I'm shocked to learn that you drink alcohol," I said with a confused look on my face.

Edweird's eyes quickly widened, as if he had just been caught with his hand in a cookie jar. "What was I *thinking*? You know, you are completely right. How silly of me! I'm such a silly guy, a silly-nilly.

Just call me Silly-nilly-Eddie, the silly nilly with a silly willy!"

I kind of wish he had not said that. It was awfully embarrassing to hear him talk that way.

"So, just bring me any beverage," he said to the waitress. "But make sure it's red. I like red. Red rhymes with Fred, as in Flintstones. Yabba-Dabba-Doo!"

"That's super, Eddie." Mabel said, her eyes widening as well. "I'll be back with your drinks shortly." She then spun and slowly walked away.

Edweird followed her strut until she disappeared into the kitchen. He then turned his gaze back to me.

"How ya' doing, pretty girl? You've had one heck of an evening."

"I'm fine," I said, mesmerized once again by Edweird's perfection. His dazzling eyes were particularly dazzling this evening.

As I gazed at the loveliness that was Edweird, it suddenly struck me that I had paid so little attention to his attire—not just tonight, but pretty much the whole time we were together. I know that's a pretty odd thing for anyone to miss, especially a girl, but I could not for the life of me tell you one thing that he had worn before this moment. Except that red-lined black cape I saw him in one night—but I digress. Anyway, Edweird was wearing this oh-so-sweet looking polyester-suede blend jacket with wide lapels and big yellow smiley faces plastered all over the front. On one arm was a picture of Hannah Montana, and on the other was an original autograph from Vincent Price. On the back of the jacket was a cryptic message written in script: "Keep on Truckin!" Under his jacket, Edweird was wearing a torn, dingy yellow t-shirt, circa the Nixon administration. He also had on some baggy sweat pants, black socks and those fancy open-toed sandals. I suppose he was making a statement with his clothes, but I had no idea what he was trying to say. I was a little afraid to ask, if you want to know the truth, and even more afraid of the answer.

"You know," I began to say after a long, uncomfortable pause, "I'm still trying to figure you out. *Who is* Edweird Sullen? What's his story? What makes him tick?"

"That sounds like a line from a movie I saw fifty years ago," Edweird said, and then his eyes widened and moved side to side. "Oops, forget I said that."

I looked at him quizzically. "There's something different about you, I just can't put my finger on it. But I'm going to figure this mystery out, one way or another."

I could tell that my comments made Edweird a little uncomfortable. He was always in control around me, but my probing into his inner being was making him nervous. He put his index finger in his mouth and instinctively began massaging his tiger-like incisors.

"Haven't we had this conversation before? Didn't you raise this topic when you were in the hospital?" Edweird asked.

"Maybe, but I still haven't gotten a straight answer from you. I've seen enough of you to know that you are not like other boys."

"Is that so? Well then, do you have any *new* theories about me, Stella? Once again, I'm all ears."

"Yes, I do have some new theories about you." I sat up in my chair, and leaned back slightly. "And here they are, in random order: First, you own some sort of police scanning equipment. That much I'm sure of. I mean, how else would you have known that I was in trouble tonight? Second, you are older than you let on—two or three years, tops. Third, you have some dark secrets, and you aren't exactly who you seem to be. But I don't know who, or what. Perhaps you were a child actor, or even a stunt double? The Queen of Scots? Were you a witness to the birthing of baby Jesus? Perhaps it was *you* who parted the Red Sea, hmmm? Or maybe you're a TV repairman, or a toll booth attendant? Have you ever spent time digging for gold, climbing the highest mountains in a string bikini, or walking people's dogs for extra cash? Are you some kind of hustler, a pool shark maybe? I could also see you as a conniving salesman selling expensive vacuum cleaners to naïve homeowners with hardwood floors. Do you work in a factory putting tops on toothpaste tubes? Maybe you stomp wine grapes for a living, or sell vitamin tonic on late night infomercials. Have you worked in a nuclear power plant, a bowling alley, or as an astronaut on the space shuttle? I can see you as a real estate agent, an architect wannabe, or an executive for the New York Yankees. I bet you've worked as an editor, a copywriter for a clothing catalogue, and a personal assistant to wealthy businessman. Are you a standup comedian? Or just a crazy neighbor who pops in and out of a scene from time to time? Those are just some of my theories. Am I getting warm, Edweird?" I said coyly, knowing that I was dangerously near the truth.

Edweird stared at me in utter disbelief. His eyes glimmered, twinkling like the brightest stars in the universe. "Stella, I adore you, and your amazing theories about me."

He took a small sip of his drink. "Let's, hypothetically, say that I am a little different than most people you know. Would that really matter to you? Would you look at me differently than you do now? Would you think less of me if I weren't exactly who you thought I was?

"Of course not, Edweird," I said resolutely. "I feel a bond between us. I feel like you are my guardian angel, my personal bodyguard who's always looking after me. Like Kevin Costner in *Water World*."

"I feel the same way too, Stella." Edweird said. "My heart starts to tremble whenever you're around. I lose control. I try to fight it, but I can't. I haven't felt this way in fifty years. I mean *five* years. I meant to say 'five.'"

"I feel the same way too." I said. "But why are you fighting it? Why won't you just let yourself go? Open yourself up to the possibility of...love."

"It's complicated, Stella. One day I'll explain it all to you. But don't hold your breath."

Before I could say anything else Mabel returned to our table carrying our food and drinks. She placed my dinner plate and beverage in front of me, then handed Edweird a virgin Bloody Mary. Edweird didn't mind spending four times the price for what was essentially plain tomato juice because he was so tickled by the name. (He later told me, "The first time

I heard the name 'virgin Bloody Mary' I laughed so hard I wet my pants. God's honest truth.")

"Is there anything else I can get you?" Mabel asked, directing her question to Edweird.

"He took a big gulp of his Bloody Mary then casually wiped the trail of juice pouring down his chin. "No, that should do it for now. Thanks."

"Perhaps some dessert then? A little coffee, a little tea…or maybe, a little…*me*?"

"Ooh baby, that sounds great!" Edweird said all excited until he noticed me glowering at him. "I mean, uh, the lady will have some coffee. Coffee sounds great. Good ol' great coffee. Love that coffee. Caffeine rocks!"

"Actually, I'll pass on the coffee." I said to the waitress. "Now, off you go."

I ate my dinner in silence, thinking about all the things that Edweird was *not* telling me. Edweird, on the other hand, was hard at work on the coloring book the restaurant provides for little kids. He colored at an amazing pace, and with the artistry of Michelangelo. Not a single stroke of crayon had gone outside the thick line, and his "Clown Holding Balloons" masterpiece was completed in less than four minutes. After signing his picture he put the four crayons back in their cardboard box and neatly secured the lid.

"Oh, I forgot to mention," he said, "I'm going hunting with my family this weekend. So, I won't be able to see you for a couple of days."

"Wow, you guys are always off hunting together. You must really enjoy murdering helpless, innocent

Stephen Jenner

animals. Are you going to bring home lots of game to store for the winter?" I asked.

"No, we pretty much consume everything we kill, right then and there. Not the meat, of course, we just toss that away. We drink all the blood, though; two or three gallons, I imagine. Not a drop left behind."

Hoookay. Right. I think it's time for me to revise my theories about him.

"Okay, Edweird, it's time that we talk. I mean *really* talk. No more games. I'm not leaving this restaurant without a true understanding of who—or *what*—you really are."

"I've already heard all your theories about me, Stella. I find them quite entertaining."

"I'm delighted to hear that." I said. "But there's still one theory I haven't shared with you. I'm going to give it to you straight, and I'm going to need a straight answer in return."

Edweird sat up in his chair. "Fair enough. Let's have it."

I had all but run out of theories about Edweird. All that was left were the legends about werewolves and vampires Yakob had told me that night in La Shove. I knew that these tales about the Sullens being vampires were a reach, but it was all I had. So I began to tell Edweird everything that Yakob had said and danced.

"Exactly who told you these fantastic stories?" Edweird asked.

"The boy's name is Yakob Brown. He's actually a friend of mine. He's done a lot for me."

"Is that right?" Edweird said, sounding a little jealous and suddenly interested in what I had to say. "So tell me, what can Brown do for you?"

"If you must know, he can fix trucks very well. He's a very good listener, and he can tell me stories through both the spoken word and interpretive dance."

"You can't be serious!" Edweird said. "Are you telling me that he performed an interpretive dance for you? For *free*? Hell, I must have paid fifty bucks a ticket last summer for the live interpretive dance performance of *A Street Car Named Desire*. Stella! You have no idea how lucky you are."

"Well, the funny thing is, Yakob's performance was about the Sullens." I said. I took a deep breath. "Specifically, his dance told the story of how the Sullens were all ...vampires."

Edweird, who inexplicably had been downing large quantities of water, spewed out the contents of his mouth onto the busboy. "He said *what*?!?"

"I seem to have hit a nerve, Eddie," I said, knowing that I had just hit a nerve. "So it's true, isn't it? The whole lot of you—vampires? Of course! It all makes perfect sense now. It explains *everything*. You *crave* me; you yearn for me, and you can barely contain yourself from killing me—that's why you love me and hate me all at the same time. You can read minds, just like the vampires do in all those Ed Wood movies. And you're the complete package, perfect in every way, just like the vampires I have always read about. No human male can compete with you. That's why girls and women of all ages swoon all over you. Hell, if someone wrote a book about you, well, it'd sell a million copies the day it was released. And if someone else was clever enough to write a parody—you know, to provide some comic relief during these extremely difficult economic times—that would probably be an even bigger seller, or at least it should be. So, just come clean with me, Ed. Your secret's safe with me, and whoever reads my internet blog. You...are...a...vampire!"

Edweird stared back at me, and then lowered his eyes. His body language told the whole story. I nailed it; I finally got one over on him. I had captured his king. Check and mate.

"You finally got it right, Stella," he confessed. "You are right about me, about my family, and my universal appeal to all women both great and small. And you are especially right about the parody. It *would* be a shame if that baby didn't sell a couple million copies in its first year. A real shame."

Our conversation was interrupted by our waitress who had just returned and placed the bill in the middle of the table. Edweird coolly slid it toward me.

"Hey," he said, "You can at least let me pay the tip. What's four percent of eighteen bucks?"

Edweird and I gathered our things and walked to his car to begin the drive back home. Other than his incessant "knock-knock" jokes we barely spoke a word. As he turned into my driveway I noticed that he was in deep thought. I imagined that he was thinking about how I now knew the truth about him. But, then again, I also knew that he spent several hours every evening thinking about which breakfast cereal he would *like* to have had the next morning if food wasn't completely off limits to his delicate digestive system. So, I really wasn't sure what he going on in that perfect head of his. Edweird turned off the engine and looked innocently into my eyes.

"What you said back there in the diner—is it really true? I mean, all of it?"

"Yes, Edweird. Every bit."

"But you said nothing about full length feature movies. I mean, if you're telling me that books about me would sell like hot cakes, then wouldn't a lucrative movie deal naturally follow?"

"Are you kidding? Of course! And even before that people would make up their own movies trailers and put them on Youtube. And don't get me started on internet web sites and discussion groups dedicated solely to *you*. Of course, this is all a wild guess on my part, but I'm usually right about these things."

"And what makes you think you're right about this?" Edweird challenged.

"Well, let's just say a little…*swan*…whispered in my ear." I winked at Edweird, who seemed to completely miss the reference. It just goes to show you: You DO end up marrying your father after all.

I got out of the car and Edweird started up the engine. "Good night, Stella," he said to me as he started to drive away.

"Good night, Edweird," I whispered back. "Don't let the werewolves bite."

9. INTO THE WOODS

THE NEXT MORNING I was making breakfast for Harley when I heard him tumble down the stairs. He walked over to the kitchen rubbing his head and plopped himself in a chair.

"You okay, Harley?"

"Yeah, I'll be all right," he said. "I wish someone would put a sign up there warning me about the stairs. I'll get one of my boys at the station to look into this."

"Good idea, dad."

Harley started eating his cereal and toasted English muffin and went right to work on the Jumbo puzzle found in the daily newspaper. "I wish they'd put the answers on the same day instead of making us wait a day," he complained.

I nodded.

"Hey Stella, are you going to the school dance tonight? I bet there are lots of boys who would just love to take you. And a few girls, too. Did you know I met your mother at a dance? It was the homecoming dance, back in 1985. She was all dressed up in a red…no…white…hmm, what was she wearing? A tuxedo? No, that can't be right. Wait, wait. It wasn't the homecoming dance, and it wasn't your mother, it was our school trip to an abandoned coal mine. I was seventeen years old and…"

"I'd love to stay and hear the rest of the story, Harley, but I can't. To answer your question, no, I am not going to the dance. I have a school report due next week, so Maria and I are heading to the library all day to work on it. I'll be back late."

"You've once told me a story about this so-called 'library.' That's the place that allegedly lets you borrow books for free, right?"

"Right, Harley."

"Well, then, you go do what you have to do. I'm staying home today. I'll have a date with the Olson twins. There's a *Full House* marathon and I don't want to miss a minute."

"You have fun with that, Harley. I'll catch up with you later."

I didn't like to lie to Harley, but sometimes it was necessary. I was not headed to the library today. I had plans to spend the day with Edweird. I can't tell you what the plans are because he kept them a secret from me and I couldn't get a single clue out of him. The only thing he said was to dress comfortably, bring my hiking boots, a canteen filled with water, some bug spray, a compass, and enough food rations for a day. That Edweird, he was so mysterious.

I heard a car pull into the driveway and the horn honked. That was the sign. Edweird had arrived.

"Off to the library, Harley. Have a nice day!"

I ran outside the house and stumbled down the slippery stairs. After regaining my balance I walked over to my truck and jumped in the passenger side. Today I would ride shotgun. Edweird then got out of his car and hopped in the driver's seat. He would drive. Our plan was working to perfection.

"Harley said it'd be a nice day today," I shouted to Edweird so he could hear me over the loud clap of thunder and pouring rain.

"Nice day for a *fish*," Edweird added, his attempt at humor falling way short.

Edweird pulled the truck out of the driveway and headed toward the freeway. He still hadn't given me any indication where we were headed, however, I had a sense that it had to do with that nature crap—you know, hiking, climbing, wildlife, and maybe a ride on his back through the forest. Who knows? How could anyone know what to expect with Edweird, the self proclaimed "Great Northwestern Man of Mystery"?

"Cap'n Crunch!" Edweird blurted out for no particular reason.

"*Excuse me*?" I said.

"I've given it a tremendous amount of thought, Stella. If I could eat any breakfast cereal in the world, it would be Cap'n Crunch. Golden Grahams was a close second, though. But the fact that the crunch berries turn red in milk really sealed the deal for me."

"I think you made the right choice, Edweird." I said reassuringly.

Edweird smiled broadly, and then his expression became a little more serene. "So, Harley thinks you'll be at the library working on your science project?"

"Right," I said. "Except I'm not sure Harley even believes that libraries exist. He's certainly never seen one, let alone been to one. I imagine he'll have the boys back at the station look into this, but I think it'll be all right."

"Then it sounds like a plan, Stan," Edweird said. I really hated when he talked like that.

We drove for what seemed like hours, but in actuality was just a couple hundred minutes. For the latter part of the trip we were far off the beaten path. Our journey had taken us to a dirt road that appeared to be seldom used. Perhaps the occasional hiker, or the mafia dumping off a body, would travel down this way. But to the rest of the world, this road didn't even exist.

And just like that the road ended. We would travel no farther, at least not by truck. I was hoping there was some kind of taxi or shuttle service available to take us to our final destination, but that was not the case. It had become clear to me that our journey—wherever it would take us—would be done on foot. Well, two feet.

Edweird and I got out of the truck and stretched our arms and legs. He took a few steps forward, pivoted toward me and spread his arms wide.

"Welcome to Fantasy Forest!" Edweird proudly announced. His words were slightly drowned out, however, by the sound of a jet liner flying over our heads. Edweird pointed to the sky and excitedly shouted, "The plane! The plane!"

The rain had stopped and that bright, hot gaseous ball in the sky made a rare appearance. I took off my "Dora the Explorer for President" sweatshirt Harley had bought me for my 16th birthday and wrapped it around my waist. Edweird took off his Transylvania University sweatshirt and wrapped that around his waist as well. I always thought it was kind of queer for a guy to do that, but that's just me.

"So, have we arrived at the place where we'll have our picnic, and not have to hike at all?" I asked wishfully.

"Not exactly, Stella. I'm not that kind of fella." Edweird replied, just to tick me off. "This is no day at the spa. Today we go hiking, whether you want to or not. Over the next several hours you will be challenged physically, mentally, and emotionally like you've never been before."

I shuddered at the thought. There was no doubt in my mind that I would die here.

"But before we go," Edweird continued, "let's pause for a moment so you can admire my amazing physique. Take it away, Stella."

I could barely concentrate on what Edweird had just said to me. I was completely distracted by his Adonis-like physique. His skin-tight shirt, buttoned nearly to the top, had perfectly framed and accentuated his muscular man-boobs. His cutoff jeans, circa 1970, did little to conceal his ripped hips, thighs and buttocks. The stubble from his freshly shaven chest danced like raindrops off his cool white skin. At this very moment, I wanted him more than I ever wanted any other man, and nearly every other woman.

"Um, are you finished gawking at me, Stella?" Edweird asked with a sly smile.

"Uh, sure," I replied. "At least for *now*."

"Good. We better get an early start on our hike, so I don't have to carry you on my friggin' back before it gets pitch black."

"You know, I'm not a strong hiker," I admitted. "I don't know how far I can make it. Perhaps I'll just stay in the car while you go off and strut your stuff in the woods for an hour or so."

"Stella, you're such a downer. You're bringing me down." Edweird was clearly losing his patience with me. "Look, it's not like you're some fat chick who can't walk a mile without passing out or having to stop at Denny's for their lunch buffet. You've got two perfectly good legs that can get you from point A to point B, like a trusty old truck. And you've got *me*. What else could a girl need? Enough of your whining, Crow. Let's get this godforsaken hike started so we can get the hell out of here."

"Fine."

We started on our hike a little before noon. Although it was starting to warm up the densely shaded path made the air feel cool and rather pleasant. After a couple miles I was actually surprised how well I was progressing. I was equally surprised how much Edweird was *struggling* to keep up. Though his physique was impressive to look at, it clearly did not translate to athleticism. For instance, any time our path was blocked by a fallen tree or a large, dead animal, it was *me* who had to lift *him* over the obstruction. My impression of him certainly was not bolstered when he giggled like a school girl as I heaved him over the last boulder. Honestly, the whole hiking experience thus far kind of took him down a notch or two.

We hiked mostly in silence, which allowed me to enjoy the natural beauty enveloping us. Mostly by default, I ended up being the pace setter. Occasionally Edweird would make simple yet sometimes awkward conversation—inquiring about my 401(k) retirement plan or any undisclosed mental illness of mine that he should know about. Every so often he'd fake an injury as his way of attempting humor, but I found that rather annoying. He also kept asking "Are we there yet?" every few hundred feet. I think he was serious about that, though.

After three hours of hiking, the path led us to a magnificent pasture, with spacious skies, amber waves of grain, purple mountains majesties, above the fruited plain. Smack dab in the middle was an abandoned multicolored school bus, circa 1971, that I'm guessing once belonged to the Partridge Family. I wasn't sure what the Partridges had been doing in vampire country, but maybe that would explain Laurie Partridge's unusual eating habits. Edweird, energized by our arrival, emphatically flung his shirt off like he had just scored the winning goal in the women's 2000 World Cup finals. His shiny skin was soaking up the sun when he noticed me gawking at him, prompting a coy smile.

"Would you like to take a moment to describe to your readers how perfect I am—even more perfect then before?" he asked.

"You betcha!"

Okay, here we go again. Edweird's perfection was even more perfect than it was this morning, as he suggested. His beauty dwarfed that of Adonis, Endymion, Narcissus, and Hyacinthus. His wind-swept hair was standing on end, as if screaming to the heavens and challenging the Gods to send down an angel whose locks could rival his own. Rubies, emeralds and diamonds appeared grimy and worthless when Edweird fluttered his jeweled eyes. His glistening platinum skin re-directed the sun's rays back to the stars, creating a rainbow over Jupiter's second moon. As he walked his left and right pectorals danced the perfect tango, knocking down trees that foolishly dared to stand in his way. Noble kings and princes would bow when'er he came. Pirate ships would lower their flags when Puff roared out his name.

"I gotta pee," Edweird announced, breaking this perfect moment. "When I get back I need to ask you a question."

Edweird disappeared into the woods, and a moment later, made it unmistakably clear that he was feeling quite relieved. He returned and walked up next to me.

"Sometimes I come here by myself to get away from it all, to think, to just be alone," he said. "Light up a doobie. You know, just hang."

"It's lovely, Edweird. It's absolutely perfect." I picked up a stick and began scraping away the deer poop embedded in my boots.

Edweird gazed down at me, his eyes darker than normal. His look was no longer welcoming, but more focused. I felt him examining my face, studying my expression, reading my mind. I no longer felt like his companion. I felt like his prey.

"I scare you, Stella, I can feel it. I can taste it. You are frightened by me. I'm sorry."

"No, Edweird, that's not true," I lied. I was feeling pretty darned scared.

"Stella, what is it that frightens you?" he asked.

I had to pause for a moment to collect my thoughts. "Quite a few things, actually. I am frightened of the unknown. I am frightened of the known. I get creeped out by snakes, firecrackers, and mysterious bugs in my soup. Also by snakes in my soup, firecrackers in bugs, and mysterious soup in general. By meteor showers during the day, and by global warming at night. That loud noise coming from the truck's engine scares the bejesus out of me. Oh, the boogie man, too. And sharks. Those are a few of my least favorite things."

"Interesting," Edweird said. "But what about *me*? What is it about me that frightens you?"

"Gee, I don't know," I said, with a hint of irony in my voice. "For starters, you're a century-old vampire in the guise of a boy who can't seem to finish high school. You live with other vampires who you pretend are your relatives and the bunch of you get your jollies by hunting and killing wild animals with your bare hands. And I'm pretty sure you've killed an innocent person or two, or maybe a werewolf in your day. So, come on, if *that's* not a bit spooky, then I don't know what is."

"Anything else?" Edweird inquired.

"I've barely scratched the surface. But let's just leave it at that, shall we?" I said.

"Very well."

Edweird didn't seem the slightest bit put off by my honesty. He appeared to be taking all of this in at once. What seemed like a very long ten seconds—or an incredibly short twelve seconds—passed before either one of us spoke. Edweird's belch broke the silence. After waving his hand in front of his mouth, and questioning where that burp came from, his expression turned more serious. He then reached in his hip pocket and thumbed through a tiny book.

"You know, Stella," he said, "there's this unseen, invisible, transparent, and undetectable tension between us. It's barely discernable, and virtually impossible to perceive." Edweird closed his mini thesaurus and shoved it back in his pocket.

I nodded slowly in agreement.

"So," he continued, "maybe it's time we break the tension between us. Howsabout a big smooch right on the old kisser?" Edweird said with a silly grin on his face.

Edweird's words made my heart skip a crazy beat. I had imagined this moment since I was a little girl, playing with my Ken, Barbie, and Count Dracula dolls. Ken would run off with his friends to some sleazy bar, and Dracula was always there to comfort the love-starved Barbie. The next thing you know, Barbie and Dracula were redecorating the ol' dollhouse, while Ken was looking for his next fix. And now, I was Barbie, and Edweird was the brave little vampire. The moment was here, the time was right. I would finally kiss my century-old dream boy.

"Edweird, if this does happen, things will be different from this point on—for you and for me. Once you've had an ungainly waif, there's no going back."

"I don't want to go back, Stella. I want you. I promise I do."

"You're not the first boy to make promises to me, Edweird." I said. "There have been dozens of boys who've told me the exact same thing. And I believed them all. The high school quarterback, the milkman, the wide receiver, the teacher's assistant, the lion tamer, the place kicker and school principal to name a few. Sure, we dated a few times. But did they ever call me back? Send me a page? Text message? Email? Carrier pigeon? Smoke signals? Message in a bottle? No, no, no, no, no, no. And no. So, don't start trying to smooth talk me into being your girlfriend if you don't really mean it, because I don't want to get hurt no more. I got feelings. You think you're good enough for *this*? 'Cause you got to show me somethin.' If talk is all you got, then talk to the hand."

My admonishment had completely caught Edweird by surprise. His eyes were now closed, and he was doing a magnificent impression of an old man snoring. A minute passed and his snoring grew louder. Perhaps he had, in fact, nodded off for a moment. I gave him a firm push.

Edweird's entire body jolted. "I don't like clowns! Make them go away!" he shouted. His eyes fluttered open and beads of sweat had formed over his brow. His expression quickly went from desperation to relief as he realized the traveling circus was only in his dreams.

"So?" I asked, "What do you have to say for yourself?"

"Um, what you just said…I understand…and I agree with …I think…Sure, what the heck."

"Oh, Edweird!" I gushed. "You *do* understand me. You're not like the others, I just know it. I knew it all along. We'll have lots of babies, and you can get a job as a midnight watchman at the DQ, and I'll stay home and make cookies and try not to burn the place down. It'll be so wonderful. I can't wait to tell dad!"

"Whoa, slow down there, Better Crocker," he retorted. "You're taking this a few steps too far. I was just thinking of getting to first base with you, nothing more. Stella, you must remember this, a kiss is still a kiss, a smile is just a smile."

"Not to me it isn't!" I protested, perhaps a little too much.

"Let's not complicate things, Stella. I was just thinking a little peck on the cheek. I'll press my cold, hard, Elgin marble lips against your warm, soft, moist, voluptuous ones. And lean my gleaming white, rock hard chest up against you, my hands feeling the warmth of your body, stroking your side, working their way down to your hips and thighs, to their final destination of your left and right buns. Something real innocent-like."

His words left me breathless. Literally. The lack of oxygen to my brain made me dizzy, and I started to faint. As quickly as I did, Edweird's arms reached out to catch me, but he was too slow, and I fell painfully to the ground. Seconds later Edweird was kneeling next to me, caressing my hair with one hand, while pinching my nose and trying to stop the massive blood flow with his other. It was not quite the perfect moment I had dreamed of, but then again, he was turning out to be far from the perfect guy.

"Kiss me, Edweird!" I said, my voice forceful and demanding. "Kiss me like you really mean it. Kiss me like you've never kissed a woman before."

"Okay."

Edweird gently brushed away the dried blood from my face. He leaned over to me and began nuzzling my hair. His right hand gently caressed my cheek. His cool breath danced off my neck. I felt his teeth nibbling at my ear lobe, breaking the delicate skin. His hands gripped my upper arms, forcing them back and causing substantial bruising that would take days to heal. He then moved both his hands to the side of my face, squeezing it tight. He seemed genuinely tickled at how my scrunched lips formed that *fish face*, and whispered that I was his "Little Flat Faced Flounder Girl."

Edweird's eyes softened. He pulled my face to his and his lips found mine. His lips were even colder than I imagined. How cold? Well, let me put it this way: Have you ever stuck out your tongue and pressed it to a frozen flag pole? And an instant later, it's pretty much stuck and you're like, "I made a *big* mistake" because you're quite certain that you won't ever be able to dislodge yourself without causing major tissue damage? Kind of like that. Nonetheless, I probably got you thinking that this kiss would have been miserable, but seriously, who are we fooling? If you were paying attention, you would have realized that pretty much everything Edweird does is perfect, or at least way better than any mundane human can pull off. Humans suck!

From the moment our lips touched my world was forever changed. I immediately resented all 'normal' people for being so inadequate in every way, at least compared to Edweird. I cursed the God of Abraham, Isaac and Jacob for keeping him away from me for so long. I pleaded with Vishnu and Allah to give me more arms to hold him, touch him, squeeze him. And most of all, I really wish I had a breath mint or two I could discretely shove down his throat to take the edge off his rancid breath. You'd think that of all people, vampires would be particularly concerned with oral hygiene, but not this guy. His breath reeked of the dried blood and rotting flesh of the last several dozen wild creatures he'd drained. My eyes started to water.

Edweird's lips ravaged mine for several minutes, and then he gently pushed me away. He stared at me for a moment, and I could see in his eyes he was searching for the perfect thing to say. Edweird was so worldly, so sophisticated in all things of, or pertaining to, love. I knew that he wouldn't just try to sweet talk me. He was looking for words to make me feel even more like a finely tuned love machine than I already was. But before he could speak I opened myself up to him.

"Edweird, I have a confession to make. I really like you. Not just *like*, but *like-like*. I may even be falling in love with you."

Edweird had that queer expression on his face, kind of like a golden retriever who so desperately tries to understand you, but just can't. But you love them even more for trying.

"Stella, I just don't know what to do about you," Edweird sighed. "I pride myself in being in control of every situation. But I don't feel that way with you. I feel the opposite. What's the opposite of being in control? Oh, yeah, I feel *out* of control. Or not in control. Some type of preposition that suggests that I don't have full control. That's the way I feel. Oh, I also feel a little parched. Quite frankly, I could use a stiff drink right now." He started searching under the leaves for a stray squirrel or chipmunk to take the edge off.

"Love is not about being in control, Edweird. Love is about losing control, opening up, and making yourself vulnerable. Love is about giving up so much but getting even more in return. And that's what love is all about, Charlie Brown."

"I never thought about it like that, Stella." Edweird said slowly. You've given me quite a bit to think about. My head is spinning right now. As you know, I'm normally a man of action, but I'm going to need some time to sort through all of this."

"I don't see the need to delay our true destiny any longer than we already have, Edweird." I said. "And I don't want to waste another minute not being with you. Besides, I'm not getting any younger."

"Me neither," Edweird said. "Of course, I'm not getting any older either. Yeah, baby!" He stood up and did that annoying little dance with his arms making circles in front of his gyrating hips.

"Well then, perhaps we should just take a break and have a little fun for a while." I suggested. "It would be a shame to miss out on all this beauty surrounding us."

"I was just thinking the same thing." Edweird replied, looking very relievced.

We spent the next few hours together enjoying all that nature had to offer. Edweird caught some butterflies with his bare hands and showed me how to tie their antennas into a knot. We also went apple picking in the orchard by the lake, built a wooden tool shed, went on a three-mile cattle drive and hoed ten acres of land. Edweird insisted that we play several games of "duck, duck, goose" and took it pretty hard when I won the final game in sudden death overtime. After my victory dance, he said that he needed to be alone for a while and climbed up into an old tree house.

By the time Edweird finished his sulking it was late afternoon and we only had a couple more hours of daylight. We decided to gather our things and start our hike back to the truck. Edweird was worried that it would be dark before we made it back, and insisted that we run the whole way. I knew that there was no way I could keep up with him.

"I won't be able to make it to the truck before it gets dark, Edweird. Maybe we can just take our time and walk by the light of the moon. It would be so romantic."

"Are you serious?" he said. "Do have any idea of what type of wildlife roams these woods at night? Actually, I have no idea either. But I can't imagine it's good."

"Well, what do you suggest then?" I asked.

"There is one thing. I could carry you on my back. I'll haul you back to the truck. We'll get there in no time, flat."

I wished he had chosen another the word besides "haul." It kind of makes me feel like a whale.

I was too tired and achy to argue with Edweird. He crouched down and beckoned me to hop on his back, and I obliged. He then reached back with his magnificent arms to secure me tight against his muscular back. Then, without warning, Edweird took off down the path at an amazing speed. Everything I looked at was a blur to me. Apparently, it was all a blur to him as well. He was in as much control as Helen Keller after ten cent beer night. After two hundred yards we ended up crashing into several trees and what we believed was a water buffalo. Remarkably, even with the high-speed collisions Edweird still managed to remain upright. He then repositioned me around to his front so that I would functionally serve as a human battering ram for whatever object he'd run us into next. After another fifty yards of more of the same he gave up entirely on this plan. He lowered me back to the ground, and we walked the rest of the way glowering at each other long into the night.

We finally reached the truck just before ten o'clock. Edweird and I drove back to my house in relative silence. From time to time he would nod off; fortunately I was able to reach over and grab the steering wheel in time to keep us safely on the road. We arrived at my house around midnight and found Harley snoring loudly on the couch. On TV, the Olson twins were doing something unbelievably stupid and not the least bit funny, yet the studio audience roared its approval nonetheless. It's a good thing Harley had fallen asleep. The last time he went on a Olson twins bender he ended up with a dislocated larynx from laughing too hard.

"I had a wonderful time with you, Edweird." I said. "I wish this day would never end."

"You mean one long Sunday—for all eternity? That's utterly ridiculous! When would people go to work? Nothing would ever get done. The economy would fall completely apart. It would be The Great Depression all over again, but much, much worse! I can't live through those times again, Stella. I just won't do it."

"I mean spending time with you, silly," I explained.

"Oh, I get it," Edweird said, looking very relieved. "You had me worried there for a minute."

"So, when will I see you again?" I asked, gently running my fingers over his icy cold hands.

"I don't understand your question, Stella. I mean, I'm standing right here, right now. I guess the simple answer would be: *one second from now.*"

"No, Edweird. I'm asking when you and I will be able to spend some quality time together. Maybe I can come over tomorrow and do your laundry, or we can just hang out by the Dairy Queen. I just want to be a tiny part of your life—twenty-four seven, three sixty-five."

"Hmm, good question." Edweird said, rubbing the stubble on his chin. "I've got an idea. Why don't you come over to my house and spend a few days with my family? I think it's time that they finally meet you. Does that sound good to you, Stella?"

"It sounds wonderful! I can't wait!"

"Then it's settled. I'll pick you up tomorrow, and we'll take it from there," he said.

"I'll be packed and ready first thing." I said. "I'll just need to feed Harley another lie, and we'll be on our way."

"Sounds like a plan," Edweird said. He then reached down and grabbed my hands, and his perfectly cold lips gently pressed softly against my warm cheek… ah heck, I'm just too tired to ramble on right now.

I watched Edweird hop in his car and drive away. I started to think that this was all a big mistake.

10. MEET THE SULLENS

THE NEXT MORNING Edweird met me at the front door. I had my suitcase packed and was ready to go. Harley was still passed out on the couch gripping his Oscar the Grouch blanket. I left him a note explaining that I would be spending a few days at Maria's house, working on our school project. Harley's years as Sporks' Finest had taught him nothing about deception. He would buy my story—hook, line and sinker.

Edweird and I walked from my house to his car. Having only tripped once, I felt particularly proud of myself. He escorted me to the passenger side door and said, "I'll drive."

Edweird opened the door for me and I hopped in, striking my head on the doorframe but pretending it didn't hurt. It hurt like hell. He then walked to the driver's side, opened the door, and adroitly slid onto the seat directly behind the steering wheel, managing to avoid striking any part of his body against the car. How anyone could do all those things and not injure himself, I'll never know. He amazed me to no end.

"The road to my house can be very tricky," he said, "and I don't have to tell you that women drivers as a whole stink awfully bad and you are particularly uncoordinated. So I figure it's just best for me to take control."

Though everything he said was undeniably chauvinistic and extremely insulting, it was, nonetheless, mostly true. He had a way of addressing sensitive areas with the grace of a drunken sailor.

The first thirty minutes we spent together were mostly uneventful. We saw the trees beginning to bud. We saw children playing in the street, enjoying the mild temperatures and perpetually gloomy skies. Young lovers passed by, walking hand in hand. I had looked over at Edweird, who seemed a bit uncomfortable by public display of affection, uncertain of what level of overt affection I would be receptive to. Edweird then turned his attention back to his task at hand; that is, trying to figure out where he put the car keys. We were still parked in the driveway, and I could feel him getting anxious.

"God damn sunnuva bee!" he cried out. "Bloody hell, I just *had* them! Mother…"

"Hey, look, I found them, Edweird!" I shoved my hand between the seat and the door. I grasped the keys, which he apparently dropped when he opened the door for me.

"Gracias," he said coolly. He then inserted the key into the ignition, put the clutch in gear, and drove the car out of the driveway. We were finally on our way.

We drove to Sporks' city limits and stayed on the main road for another five miles. A short while later Edweird slowly pushed the brake pedal with his perfect right foot then rotated the steering wheel clockwise. The car responded by slowing down, and veering to the right, respectively. We were suddenly off the main road, and onto a small dirt path that was just wide enough to fit a single vehicle. I had never noticed this road before; other than the large flashing neon sign that read, "Beware! Vampire Crossing Next 5 Miles" the road was very inconspicuous. We were now headed due west, and beginning to ascend the modest mountains that framed Sporks, Washington.

We continued to drive down this road that cut through the thick forest for several miles until we came to a wide clearing. This area had no earthly business being here. In the midst of the dark, dense woods, here was this place that was so pristine. At the far end of the clearing was this beautiful and exquisitely preserved three story colonial house. In my history books I had seen similar looking houses that had been constructed in the mid nineteen hundreds for the most respected community leaders. This house was obviously built by a master builder and painstakingly maintained by every subsequent owner, each who undoubtedly poured their hearts and souls into keeping this brilliant structure in its original magnificent state. I figured a very special family lived in this majestic home.

Stephen Jenner

Edweird caught me staring dreamily at this mansion. "The house you're looking at has been abandoned for nearly a year," he said. "They moved out right after the last all night kegger we had using the blood drained from a nearby pork factory." He turned his gaze to the far right. "Our house is over...*there*."

"Where?" I asked. I tried to follow the path of his eyes, but all I could see from my vantage point was this decrepit one-story hut along the perimeter of the forest. "I can't quite see it. Is it behind that decaying shack where only a sorry, white-trash family might live? Is it tucked away just inside the woods far, far removed from that dilapidated shanty?"

"Um, not exactly. It *is* that dilapidated shanty."

"Oh," I said, disappointingly. We were both kind of embarrassed at this moment. I'm sure that Edweird would have loved to have brought me home to a grandiose dwelling where his family lived, perhaps like that architectural wonder on the opposite end of the clearing. *Why didn't they just force open the door and take over that house? It was abandoned, for Chrissake. Who would know?* I'm also sure Edweird wanted me to accept him no matter what type of dwelling he lived in. On the other hand, I could have, and should have, been less critical with my opinions, especially because I knew nothing about the inside of the house. Sure, its curb appeal left much to be desired; but inside that shack may be nearly 700 square feet of unadulterated beauty. I would reserve judgment for later.

Edweird parked his car next to the 1994 Chevy Camaro that was hoisted up on four cinder blocks. The trunk was open, and six cans of recently consumed Budweiser were scattered on the front lawn, next to a large, metal tool box.

"Looks like Casper decided to give the engine an overhaul, *again*." Edweird said, shaking his head.

We got out and walked along the muddied path leading to the front door. I found the presence of mud particularly odd since we hadn't had a good rain in over a week. A scary looking armadillo was eating the poison ivy from the garden, and didn't seem the slightest bit concerned by our arrival. Overhead a copy of "The Bridges of Madison County" was dangling precariously from the gutter on the roof of the house.

Edweird pulled open the dented screen door and pushed open the front door. I took a deep breath then stepped inside. I quickly realized that the curb appeal turned out to be the highlight of this property. Tattered furniture, circa 1970's—well, make that 1870's—occupied the living room. A large print of "Dogs Playing Poker" was hanging over the fireplace. And some type of animal—my guess is a dog or a pot bellied pig—was lapping up what was left of a spilled bottle of Jack Daniels.

The living room apparently was the gathering place of the Sullens, because most of them were huddled together here. A 19-inch black and white TV with a coat hanger for an antenna was blasting "The Family Feud" game show, and the one of the boys was yelling "good answer!" to the Clark family of Witchita, Kansas. I saw a small pile of money—

mostly tens and twenties—piled on the coffee table. This show apparently incited serious gambling among the family members.

"Hi, everybody!" I said cheerfully, perhaps a little over the top. "I'm Stella. I think you know my record."

"Hi, Stella," Malice said. She was sitting on the couch and slid a ways to her left, opening up a small space for me. "Grab a cold one and plop your sweet little behind down next to mine. Don't worry, sweetie. I don't bite."

The other siblings looked up at her all with the same bored expression on their faces. "Good one, Malice," said Edweird. "Quite original."

Just then Sesame walked in from the kitchen, holding a wooden spoon that she apparently was using to stir the large pot of Chef Boy-Ardee spaghetti she was preparing for the dog/pig. Sesame was nothing short of a stereotypical-looking Italian mama: Short, stout, perhaps a tad over five feet tall, wearing a full length apron that had a picture of a road kill armadillo and the message "You brain it, I'll drain it!" embroidered across the bottom.

"Top of the morning to ya!" She shouted out to me in an old, Irish accent. She greeted me with a wide, warm smile, giving me a quick once over. "Ah, yes, you are as beautiful as Edweird told us you were."

"That's sweet, thank you," I said. I was heartened that Edweird had felt comfortable enough to have talked about me with his parents. I already felt at home.

"Ah, Stella, you made it!" exclaimed Dr. Sullen as he entered the room.

"Yes, it's so nice to see you again, Carpile."

"Please, call me Dr. Sullen," he insisted. "And welcome to our modest dwelling. It ain't much, but it's home."

He paused for a moment then the tone of his voice became a little more serious and slightly poignant. He had a forlorn look in his eyes. "You do realize, if my patients didn't sue me on a weekly basis for medical malpractice, we'd certainly be living in a place a little better than this. But, such is life: *someone* had to finish last in his class."

His expression turned even more solemn. "Stella, do you have some lose change you can spare? Help a brother out?"

I shook my head slowly. "Sorry, I can't."

"That's cool, no biggie, no problem." Carpile shrugged, sporting a sad smile, then sat down and turned his attention to the TV.

"Hi, I'm Casper, the friendly Vamp!" called out the tallest of the Sullen kids. Casper was by far the most attractive of the Sullens—if you recall, I originally had the hots for him, and not Edweird. But Casper was already spoken for, by his sister Malice. And I can guarantee that west of the Appalachians, you just didn't hear that sentence uttered aloud.

"Edweird, where are your other siblings?" I asked.

"I'm not sure," he said. "But my guess is that Dammet and Rosaries are volunteering at the homeless shelter. Either that or they're at the dog track. They're real big into gambling."

"Oh, it's a shame I missed them. Maybe I'll see them when they get back."

Edweird and I then wandered from the living room to an adjacent room decorated with fake wood paneling and sporting trophy heads of animals they had trapped—deer, bears, Chihuahuas, poodle, kitten, and what could only be described as something resembling the dog/pig pet of theirs. Perhaps its mother? The room was also filled with several instruments—a large piano, a rusty cowbell, and a triangle. There was also a very ornate guitar stand, but I saw no sign of a guitar.

"Do you play any of these instruments, Edweird?" I asked.

"I used to play the piano, but after so many concerts at Carnegie Hall I finally gave it up, cold turkey. I hadn't picked up an instrument in a good— let's see—forty, fifty years. However, in the last year I reentered the musical realm, and have committed myself to a new, amazing instrument.

"That's so exciting!" I said. "What instrument is it?"

"Actually, the instrument has been around a long time, but has only become popular in the last fifteen to twenty years. Perhaps you've heard of it. It's called the 'air guitar'?" He looked at me expectantly.

Edweird gestured toward the empty guitar stand. "I hate taking lessons, so I'm pretty much self taught. So, yeah, I do play, but don't you go asking me to play for you, because I play for *me*. I play for myself. I play alone. I'm a loner, that's just my style. I don't need no stinkin' manager, and I don't need no groupies to hear me do my thing. This isn't about money; I'll never sell out to 'The Man.' Oh no, you'll never see my playing for anyone else but me. I would not, could not on a boat. Or with a goat. Or on a plane. *Are you insane*? I would not play here, and I would not play there. I would not play most anywhere!"

I was amazed by Edweird's ability to flawlessly quote Dr. Seuss on a whim yet completely disgrace the man's work. "Oh Edweird, play it. For me. For old time's sake. Play it, Edweird. Play the air guitar."

Edweird paused long enough to glower at me, then reached down to the guitar stand to pick up what I imagined was his air guitar, I think. "As you wish."

Edweird stood up from the bed and walked over to a small wooden cabinet next to his dresser. He opened the main door, revealing a 1972-built 8-track tape player and a stack of tapes, including *Greatest Hits from the 70's Volume 3*. He leaned over and pushed button #2, and the song, "Free Bird," began to fill the room. Edweird's eyes became fixated on some imaginary object or distant place. Then, he raised his head and he began finger picking his imaginary guitar—first slow, keeping pace with the rhythm of the song, yet adding some of his own notes—*I think*. A minute later, as the song's tempo increased, his right hand began *strumming* up and down a million miles a second. As the song reached its crescendo, his brilliantly muscular arm was now flailing in circles, revolving round and around and around, like a really tiny planet on speed. Tears began pouring from my eyes, and I think I thought I saw one running down his check. (He would later write this off as being a "runaway booger"). When the song ended and a sweat-stained Edweird collapsed onto the bed. He appeared quite pleased with his performance.

"Thank you, thank you *very much*! Edweird breathless shouted out. "You've been a wonderful audience. I love you all. Good night, Sporks!" For a loner, he really was a showman.

Edweird extended his arm, and his eyes directed me to the guitar stand. I figured he wanted me to return his instrument to its proper place, *I think*.

"Careful with that," he said. "It belonged to my grandfather."

I kind of pantomimed my way through returning his air guitar to its stand, but he seemed satisfied. I then seated myself on the bed next to him. He sat straight up, and his face turned serious.

"You know, my family knows who they hate," he said, "and they don't hate you. Not yet, at least." He paused for a moment, apparently struggling how to delicately say the next sentence. "Mom and Pop think you're all right. So, you've got a solid foot in the door. Malice and Jasper can tolerate you, too. But Rosaries and Dammet aren't big fans, and they haven't really met you yet. That's kind of funny, don't you think?"

"Not really, no," I said. "It's because I'm human, isn't it?"

"That's most of it, yes," Edweird agreed. "But you're about as graceful as a hippo, and kind of goofy, too."

Ah, my dream boy strikes again.

I frowned. I didn't want to be disliked, not by anyone, and certainly not by any of the Sullens. I wanted to be accepted by all of his family members.

And it's not like I'm someone who would jump back and forth between two boyfriends whose families are sworn enemies. I'm just not that kind of girl. That just was not my style.

"So…what should I do? I can't be around a family where thirty-three percent of the people don't want me here."

"Well," he said, "I didn't say they don't want you around. They just don't care for you one iota. But they may learn to tolerate you, in good time. I think as time goes by—maybe not today, maybe not tomorrow, but soon and for the rest of your life—they'll even begin to like you. You know, the lives of one incredibly clumsy girl and one Adonis-like vampire don't amount to a hill of beans in this crazy world. Well, *my* life does. But I think this could be the start of a beautiful friendship. Here's looking at you, kid."

"Oh, I'm so relieved to hear you say that, Edweird," I said, feeling relieved that he said that.

"You don't need to worry, Stella." Edweird said reassuringly. "Things will turn out fine, I'm quite sure of that.

"What makes you so sure, Edweird?"

"Well, for starters, Malice can see the future. And she looked into *your* future. She envisioned a time when you will be completely welcomed into our family. Not just as a full time maid cleaning the floors, doing our laundry, and slopping on a fresh coat of lead-based paint on the walls. But as one of our own. You will become a part of us with beautiful pasty white skin that's cold to the touch, soft pouty lips, and nasty pointy teeth. If you don't believe me, go ask Malice. She's ten feet tall."

"What the hell do you mean by *that*?" I queried.

"Go ask Malice, over there, standing on that ten foot ladder. Talk to her. You can ask her anything you want about the future, she sees everything. As I've said, she's already envisioned your future. And let me just say, it's not without controversy."

"What exactly are you talking about, Edweird?" I asked nervously.

"Oh, nothing to get overly worried about—just a few hiccups here and there. Mostly normal stuff—you know, some vengeful vampire tricking you into going back to Phoenix and then ambushing you. You getting pretty beaten up by him," Edweird laughed feebly. "Damn near kills you, actually. Then later you are stalked by his girlfriend who's out for revenge. What a pip she is! And then there's the time that you carelessly destroy the peace agreement between us and the Quailettes creating further animosity between vampires and werewolves. And who could forget your teenage pregnancy and premature baby that ultimately puts all of our lives in jeopardy? And don't get me started on the ridiculous name you give to that poor child. Seriously, what's that all about?"

A glaze came over my eyes. I continued to stare at him, utterly confused.

"But, beyond those minor detours, it's pretty much smooth sailing," Edweird continued. "When all is said and done, things will work out perfectly for you, of course, even though you really don't deserve it. A true storybook, ahem, quadrilogy ending."

"Wow, that all sounds incredible," I said. "But how certain is she about this? It's not written in stone. Surely we have some control of our future. *We must*. Don't we, Edweird?"

"Hmmm, that's a difficult question, Stella," Edweird said. "Actually, the question is quite easy, but the answer is difficult. I suggest you find a good psychic to help you figure that one out. You can find a reputable one on the TV infomercials after midnight. Charges are $4.99 per minute and you must be eighteen or older and have a valid credit card to call. So what are you waiting for? Call now."

"Maybe some other time, Edweird," I said. "I'll just let the future unfold without me already knowing how it will all turn out. Besides, I just love surprises."

It's times like these that I wished I kept my cell phone charged and paid my credit card bills on time.

11. CARPILE

EDWEIRD AND I SPENT THE remainder of the afternoon walking the woods surrounding the house. About six o'clock my stomach started to growl, and I realized that dinner at the Sullen house was not part of their routine. Vampires, of course, hunt and drain the blood of their prey on the spot like hungry animals, and don't sit at a table like civilized people. (Humans: one, Vampires: zero). Anyway, Sesame realized my predicament, and suggested that I eat some of the dog/pig's left over canned spaghetti. Lovely.

The rest of the Sullens had retired to their shared quarters, and Edweird and I were left alone in the living room.

"Your family is wonderful," I told him. "But there's one thing I don't understand: How did you all get to be one family, when you all have such different backgrounds?"

"It all has to do with Carpile," Edweird said. "He's the one who brought us all together many years ago. You know, he's not as young as you think."

"Is that so? How old is Carpile?" I asked, staring up at Edweird's perfect marble eyes.

"Let's see." Edweird said, looking up and apparently doing some mathematical calculations in his head. Next Tuesday is the sixth...carry the two...add one for every century...that would make him three hundred sixty-four billion years old. No, wait, that's the universe. Just three hundred sixty-four years old. Period. But he's got the body of a man half his age. He keeps himself in great shape."

"Amazing!" I exclaimed. "I didn't figure him for a day over forty, forty five tops!" I tried to keep my enthusiasm in check. I did not want to seem like a giddy little school girl amongst this remarkable family.

"Carpile is a remarkable person. Would you like me to tell you about him?" Edweird asked. "I've been working on an interpretive dance sequence describing his complete life story. It's several hours long, but I'll only charge you half price. How does a sneak preview sound to you?"

"Hmm, as good as that sounds, it's pretty late and I don't want to disturb your family. Perhaps the spoken word would be better at this time of day."

"Very well then," Edweird said. "I shall monologue the story of Carpile."

"Excellent."

"Carpile was born in the mid sixteen hundreds," Edweird began. "Of course we have no way of knowing the exact month or year he was born, but we do know he was delivered exactly at 6:52:07 a.m. His father died during childbirth—he had a heart attack in the delivery room watching his wife give birth, go figure. His mother was the daughter of a wealthy aristocrat, but she received none of her parents' inheritance when they died. Half of their riches were divided evenly between her two brothers, and the other half went to funding to scientific endeavors, such as research into werewolf pattern baldness."

"That doesn't seem fair," I said.

"No, it certainly wasn't," Edweird replied. "Please don't interrupt me again."

"Okay."

"Carpile was an only child," Edweird continued, "but had many friends and always felt like part of a big family. He also had lots of pets, both great and small. When a friend or an animal got sick or injured, Carpile loved to play doctor. He would be the one to diagnose the problem and take action to find a cure. He always kept an abundant supply of leeches, and even built a homemade trepanning set to perform handy skull drilling procedures as part of his treatment protocol. Unfortunately, the recovery rate for the suffering people and pets Carpile treated was right around zero percent, so Carpile soon would find himself without any companions and very much alone.

"That's so sad," I interjected.

"Stella. Please."

"Sorry."

Edweird continued. "Carpile always had a good head on his shoulders, and eventually received a full, three month scholarship to the London School of Human and Animal Medicine and Diesel Engine Repair. In 90 days time, he would become a certified medicine man, a healer of animals great and small, and a pretty fine auto mechanic to boot."

"That's fascinating, Edweird. Please continue."

Edweird glowered at my interruption, his lips pursed like an old woman. "Carpile withstood the rigors of the curriculum. He studied seven days a week, day and night, forgoing all activities not related to his schooling. He eventually graduated 400th in his class of 399. After graduation he set up a private practice in town."

"One day Carpile received an emergency call that a rabid bat had bitten a small child, and then injured itself while flying smack dab into a diesel-powered printing press. *A trifecta!* Carpile thought. He sprinted over to the crime scene, and immediately went to work. He poured a two liter bottle of leeches onto the child who was passed out on the ground. He then got out his monkey wrench and tightened the spring-coiled sprocket that had gotten dislodged by the bat's impact. Finally, he reached for his hand-held trepan, and was taking aim on the tiny bat's head. This spooked the bat which instinctively flew at Carpile, biting him on the throat. Carpile instantly became too ill to treat himself. Sadly, the young boy ended up dying of massive blood loss. The bat died a terribly agonizing death from becoming impaled on the rusty trepan, yet interestingly enough, Carpile made a complete recovery the next day after receiving absolutely no medical intervention whatsoever.

Edweird's eyes were now moving side to side, as if he were seated courtside at Wimbledon, desperately scouring his brain for more details about Carpile. After a while he frowned imperceptibly and blurted out, "40-Love!"

"That was a long, long time ago, in a place far, far away," Edweird continued. "So, nearly four hundred years later—yada yada yada—he's still practicing medicine and I've got a bunch of vampire step brothers and sisters. There you have it."

"Wow, what an incredible life he's had," I said. "He's done more in four hundred years than I've done in my seventeen. All of a sudden I feel so insignificant."

"You shouldn't feel that way, Stella," Edweird said. "Don't get down on yourself; you humans are just a complete and utter bore. Nothing you will ever do in your lifetime can come close to what a typical vampire has accomplished. Just learn to deal with your mundane existence, and try to move on."

"I'll try, Edweird." I said, now feeling even more depressed than before. "But what about you? I've been waiting for so long to hear your life's story. I think it's time you finally told me."

"Very well, if you insist." Edweird said. "I was born in the south side of Chicago about eighty five years ago. It was the baddest part of town. And if you go down there, you better just beware, of a man named Leroy Brown. Anyway, for the first sixteen years I lived a normal and uninteresting life, just like you. However, on my seventeenth birthday I became very sick. It might have been rabies, food poisoning, typhoid fever or the fever for the flavor of a Pringles. No one seemed to know. But I was in pretty bad shape when Carpile found me passed out in the gutter.

"Where were your parents?" I asked.

"Hmmm, good question. Last I saw them was at the Chicago Fair. We had gotten separated at the Ferris wheel and never quite met up again. I was four years old at the time, but was streetwise like a kid twice my age."

"Anyway," he continued, "Carpile brought me into his shop, and a few days later I woke up with a bucket's worth of leeches attached to me, and my head all bandaged up. He told me he was somewhat surprised I had awakened. Apparently, I was his first patient—animal or human—to survive one of his treatments. From that point on we had a special bond between us, almost like father and son. Oh, did I mention that he turned me into a vampire?"

"And your siblings? What about them?"

"Carpile had a hand in saving all of them," Edweird said, as his index finger began inching up toward his right nostril. "Let's see…Casper was nearly crushed during a tragic merry-go-round malfunction. Then came Dammet, who was attacked by a rabid hamster in a pet store. Rosaries nearly died after over indulging at a pie-eating contest. Then there's Malice, who injured herself while climbing a tree. Go ask Malice, she took a ten foot fall. Finally there's Sesame: She never was sick or anything like that. I think Carpile just knocked her up."

I could only shake my head in amazement. "Amazing."

"Indeed it is." Edweird said, looking at the Tony the Tiger clock hanging on the wall, "It's getting late. We better get a cot set up so you have something to sleep on tonight."

Edweird disappeared into the cellar. After a few minutes and a lot of cursing, he emerged holding a folded cot that was no less than a half century old. He unfolded it for me in the corner of the kitchen, kicking aside the rusty trash can to make extra room. I heard the dog/pig yelp as he shoved its bed made of torn and muddy sheets aside so that the cot was on semi-solid ground. It still rocked a bit when I pushed down on it, but seemed steady enough to hold me. Sesame marched in holding some clean linens and a black comforter she had sewn from the hair of a Siamese cat. We all said goodnight to each other. As I went to lie down I ended up banging my head hard against the oven door, and was completely unconscious until the next morning.

12. PLAY BALL!

"RISE AND SHINE, YOU SLEEPY HEAD!" a voice yelled at me from the kitchen table. I opened my eyes and saw Edweird all dressed up in a baseball uniform. This couldn't be good, I thought. The dog/pig was sitting on my chest licking itself in its nether regions. One of its eyes was trained on me, the other on a rat scurrying by the stove.

"What's going on?" I asked rubbing my eyes. "What's with the outfit?"

"Oh, I thought I had told you," Edweird said. "It's game day, baby! You know, take me out to the ball game."

"Where exactly are we going, Edweird?" I asked nervously.

"Well, the Sullens are playing baseball. Today is the monthly game between the Le Shove Wolves

Bane Lovers and the Seattle Vampire Slayers. And you get to watch."

Boy, was I relieved. If I had to run those bases or swing a bat, I'd surely humiliate myself in front of his whole family. I was very happy to be a spectator. I just needed to go and scalp some tickets and buy a six-pack of beer.

The Sullens, each one in uniform, walked to a vacant lot adjacent to their house. Casper, one of today's starring pitchers, ran ahead and took his position on the pitching mound. He did some quick muscle stretches, kicked some dirt to the side, and then waited impatiently for the rest of his family to take their positions.

"Let's go!" Casper yelled out. He was already warmed up, and was anxious to get the game started.

I had no idea that vampires loved baseball so much. Quite honestly, I had no idea why *anyone* liked the game, vampire or human. But this was no ordinary ball game. As I would soon discover, baseball, when played by vampires, turned a child's game into a beautiful ballet, performed in a sylvan field of holly intermittently stained with rancid tobacco juice and deer poop.

First at bat for the Seattle Vampire Slayers was Malice "Shark Tooth" Sullen. Throws righty, bats lefty. Her career stats were worthy of Hall of Fame consideration: Life time batting average—.415. On base percentage—616. RBI's—515. Steals—483.

"Hey, batter, batter, batter, batter! Swing, batter, swing! The batter cannot hit!" I yelled to her from the stands.

Malice glowered at me, then settled in the batter's box and focused her attention on Casper, her stepbrother/lover. All relationships were put aside when a game was being played, however, and both Malice and Casper had their game faces on.

Dr. Sullen announced "Play ball!" and the game officially began. Casper "Catfish" Sullen (career lifetime record—87 wins/46 losses, and a sizzling 2.29 ERA) was set to deliver the game's first pitch. His windup was as graceful as a drunken chimpanzee, but his delivery was pure gold. He unleashed a fastball that easily exceeded one hundred forty miles an hour. Malice took a wild swing at the pitch and missed badly. Casper's expression turned smug.

"Hey, Malice," Casper sneered, "I read your future for you, and it rhymes with 'strike three.'"

"Just throw the ball, you goddamn hairy ape," Malice retorted.

Casper grimaced. He then went into another big windup, and unleashed a pitch that was well inside. Malice had to quickly jump out of the batter's box to avoid getting hit.

"Nice ball control, Casper," Malice shouted. "I guess if you can't beat him, you hit him."

"Stop your whining and play the game," Casper said while kicking dirt at her from the pitcher's mound.

Casper leaned forward to pick up the sign from his catcher, Dr. Sullen. The great doctor ordered a fastball over the right side of the plate. Once again the ball cut through the wind at a magical speed, but this time Malice was ready for it. She swung the bat gracefully, and the loud crack left no doubt that she had made full contact. The ball sailed past Casper's right ear before he had time to react. It continued its flight into the outfield, a low line drive that seemed to never touch ground as if mocking the laws of gravity. Malice flew out of the batter's box. If you blinked you would have missed her rounding first; if you sneezed you would have missed her touching second; and, if you experienced a grand mal seizure you surely would not have seen her sliding safely into third. She quickly stood up, brushed the dirt off her pants, and glanced over at Casper, waiting for his reaction.

"Lucky, damn lucky. That's what you are," Casper said, ever the sore loser.

"Right," retorted Malice, "just like all the other times I kicked your sorry butt."

Next up was Edweird. (Life time batting average—.135. On base percentage—.178. RBI's—4. Steals—1). I stood up from my seat on the rusty metal bleachers to get a better look at him leaving the makeshift dugout. After grabbing his lucky bat, he first strolled to second base and then to the visitor's dugout. I'm fairly certain he was lost. But he eventually found his way to the batter's box with a little encouragement from his family. Edweird dug his cleats into the dirt several times then took some practice swings. He turned to the Dr. Sullen and offered to sign autographs. Edweird immediately called timeout, backed away from the batter's box, and began singing the national anthem of both the United States and Canada. He then suggested that we move up the 'seventh inning stretch' to the first inning. That suggestion was strongly vetoed by Dr. Sullen.

"Edweird, please," Casper pleaded, clearly not thrilled by the unnecessary delay.

"Just going through my routine, Casper. We ball players are very superstitious. You've got to respect that. Respect the streak, respect the game. You throw the ball, you hit the ball, you catch the ball. Now, back off and let me be."

Edweird eventually returned to the batter's box to everyone's relief. Casper then went through his windup and unloaded a curve ball, which froze Edweird in his tracks.

"Strike one!" announced Dr. Sullen, who was also serving as the games umpire.

Edweird's expression turned sour, but he regained his composure and readied himself for the next pitch. This time Casper unloaded a fastball, high and tight. Edweird's slow reaction nearly caused him to be hit on the jaw. As it was, he cried out like a wounded Chihuahua, though the ball touched him.

Casper again went into his windup a third time, and threw Edweird a slow pitch. When Edweird saw Casper release the ball he tightly closed his eyes, counted out loud "One Mississippi," and swung haphazardly. Luck was on his side, and Edweird actually made contact, sending a floater to shallow right field. Since there were only three players on each side, and right field had been left unattended, Edweird took full advantage of this opportunity. He admired his hit for a long moment then took off, moving from zero to sixty in about four seconds flat. Unfortunately, he started off running toward third base, and only after rounding second and sliding into first was he informed of his mistake. He protested being called out, indicating that he was unaware of any such rule change that required him initially to run to first base. After a heated argument Edweird finally relented and slouched his way back to the dugout.

"Edweird, you were wonderful!" I said. Clearly, it was his in his favor that I knew nothing at all about baseball. Edweird was quick to inform me that he was a hero and the others were all just sore losers.

The Sullens' game—like that of real baseball—lasted for several grueling hours. Without giving you a play-by-play, I'll let you know that things got pretty ugly. First of all, there was a two and a half hour rain delay. Once play resumed, some drunken fan (I can't remember if it was me or not, I had had quite a few beers that day) took off all her clothes and ran onto the field. There were also three—count them—three bench clearing brawls after each pitcher had intentionally hit the opposing batter. Dr. Sullen had to work overtime to patch up the injured players well enough to get them back on the field. His trepan got a full workout that day, and no less than two hundred leeches were called into service. The game mercifully ended when the sun finally set and darkness prevented this nightmare from continuing. In the end, the Le Shove Wolves Bane Lovers had eeked out a win over the Seattle Vampire Slayers, 44–42, in twenty-three innings. Edweird went hitless—a perfect zero for twenty-four.

Though everyone seemed to have enjoyed themselves, the day ended on a very serious note. First a little background: Today was "Fan

Appreciation Day," where the first three fans to arrive at the game received a free autographed picture and bat from Baseball legend and Hall of Famer Cal Ripken, Jr. Wow, I thought; that would be worth a lot of money! Since I was the first and only fan at the game, I took the liberty of taking all the souvenirs for myself. I figured I'd keep one, and sell the others on eBay for a pretty penny.

Things did not go according to plan, however. Two other fans—a young man and his girlfriend—showed up late to the game. They politely introduced themselves as Shame and Ursula. When they saw the banners declaring today fan appreciation day, they demanded that I hand over the extra Cal Ripken, Jr. memorabilia I had taken for myself. When I refused they both became extremely agitated. The two of them then barraged me with insults.

"Those souvenirs would have paid for our wedding and honeymoon!" Ursula said. I guess she also had plans to sell them and make a buck. "And now we have nothing. You just ruined our dreams!"

"You know, I'd expect a little more professional courtesy from a fellow vampire," said Shame repulsively. "Especially a rather ordinary looking one like you. How utterly disgraceful."

"Oh, you're a vampire?" I said. "Wow, I'm actually human, but my friends here are vampires, too."

"You're *human*? Shame cried out. "And the Sullens consider you a friend? This is totally unacceptable."

Our conversation caught the attention of the Sullen family, who immediately flew over to us and stood in formation in front of me. I'm no Alvin Einstein, but I had the sense that everyone here already knew each other and were not the best of friends.

"Shame. Ursula." Edweird calmly addressed the visitors. "It's so nice to see you again...*Not*! It would be so excellent if you were to leave and never come back. That would be awesome."

"We were just heading out, Eddie," said Shame. "But let me make this perfectly clear so even you can understand it. Your human pet has taken what is rightfully ours, and we plan to get it back, no matter what it takes. This is far from over, Edweird. You're all going to regret what happened here today; maybe not today, maybe not tomorrow, but soon, and for the rest of your lives."

"What is it with you vampires always quoting from *Casablanca*?" I said. "I mean, great movie and all, but give it a rest. You should really consider referencing something from *Toy Story 2* or any of the *Indiana Jones* movies—you know something a little more uplifting."

All the vampires nodded their heads in agreement.

"Goodbye, Shame," said Malice menacingly.

Shame and Ursula disappeared into the forest. The Sullens waited until there was complete silence before talking again.

"Well, this sucks," said Dr. Sullen. "Shame is going to try and kill Stella, and now we all have to risk our necks protecting her. Way to go, Stella!"

"Yeah, way to go," added Sesame, whose tone could easily have been mistaken for Lucy Van Pelt chiding Good Ol' Charlie Brown.

For some reason, I no longer felt welcome at the Sullens' place. I can't exactly place my finger on it, but I have a very keen sixth sense about these things.

13. MOMMA, CAN YOU HEAR ME?

I WOKE UP THE NEXT MORNING overhearing the Sullens discussing their strategy for protecting me, and what our vulnerabilities might be. They all agreed that I would be safe here. The greater challenge was protecting my family. They figured that Harley would be safe—he carried a gun, and quite frankly, no one would really miss him if he were gone. However, they agreed that if Shame wanted to get to me, he would probably go through my mother—not literally of course, because she was a beast—but figuratively. I suddenly feared for her life. If I stayed here, then mom would become a target. I had to warn her, and then leave this place. Besides my mother's safety, the cot I had been sleeping on was killing my back. Of course I also didn't want to put the Sullens in danger because of me. Man, I really hated that cot. I was also pretty tired of the dog/pig scooting up and down me as I slept.

I reached for the telephone and frantically pushed ten buttons, hoping that a phone in my mother's house would ring and she would be there to answer. I hadn't paid close attention to the numbers I dialed, and was a bit surprised when a woman with a thick Asian accent answered the phone.

"Rising Sun Restaurant. We cook food for you because you too lazy to cook for yourself. We not deliver, you must pick up, you lazy sloth! Can I take your order?"

"Um…yes, sure." I said, unprepared to place my order. "I'll just have an egg roll, um, with a side order of fries, a full meat gyro—please Super-size that—some curry chicken and a falafel, with extra cheese."

"Okay, that will be one hundred fifteen dollars. I charge you more because you so ugly." The woman said. "Ready in fifteen, twenty minutes. You come here and pick up…you need exercise, lazy fat girl!"

"Okay, see you soon. Thanks." I said. She was actually nicer than the local Chinese restaurant I usually go to. I hoped the food was as good as the customer service.

I tried a second time to call my mother, this time concentrating on each number as I dialed. I executed the dialing sequence to perfection. The phone rang several times but there was no answer. I figured that mom was either out of the house or away from her desk, or maybe she was screening her calls, or incapacitated due to alcohol or substance abuse, legally deaf, or had suffered multiple life threatening injuries. Or she was already dead, which would have been a real downer, but also would have saved me a road trip from hell. The answering machine eventually picked up. I listened intently to the outgoing message for the exact instructions about what I should do following the beep: *Name, date, time of call, and message* I repeated to myself, rehearsing the explicit directives.

"Mom, it's me. Stella. It's 9:16 a.m. west coast time. The following is my message, please listen and take copious notes." I had successfully gotten the preliminaries out of the way. Now it was up to me to leave a well thought out message. "This might sound a little weird, but here goes: A vampire named Shame is coming to kidnap you. He's pretty pissed off. Call me back as soon as you can. I love you! Send money. Buh Bye."

I hung up the phone. Now, all I could do is wait and pray—and perhaps find my way to the Chinese restaurant to pick up my order.

I thought about calling Harley, but I didn't want to get him involved. Though I loved him dearly, he was completely incompetent—not just as the police chief, but as a father and a human being. Besides, there was a *Dora The Explorer* marathon on TV today, and I knew that *nothing* was going to pull him away from that. Bless that cholesterol-laden heart of his.

Moments later the phone rang and Malice answered it. "Sure, she's right here." Malice handed me the phone, and said, "It's your mother, or someone who does an amazing impersonation of her.

So it's either your mom, Rich Little, or maybe Dana Carvey."

I took the phone, and spoke excitedly. "Mom? You got my message. How are you?"

"I'm fine, dear." My mother's voice replied. "Everything's fine, your step dad is doing great. The neighbors are having a picnic this afternoon, and they invited me to come over. I was thinking of bringing a fruit salad, do you think that's okay? Maybe just a watermelon, the kids all love that. Hmm, I'll have to give it some more thought. Oh, and just one more thing, sweetheart: *I'm not your mother.*"

The voice of the last sentence spoken was no longer that of my mother. It was the voice of a man, silky smooth and calm. Like a cool gentle breeze on a perfect autumn day—with a touch of Sylvester Stallone mixed in.

"Yo, Stella!" The voice continued. "I was thinking that you should act like it's your mother you're talking to. You see, you and I need to make a special arrangement, and your little vampire friends can't know what's going on. Do you think you can do that for me, Stella?"

"Sure…*mom*…whatever you say." I said. I knew exactly who it was on the other end of the phone. It was Shame, the vampire with a real attitude. But I figured since he was holding my mother hostage, he would be the one calling the shots. And if I wanted to save my mom and keep the Sullens safe, I had better listen and abide by his demands.

"Excellent, Stella," the voice continued. "I need you to keep talking to me as if I were your mother.

Can you do that for me, Stella? Stella, Stella Bo-Bella, Fe Fi Fo Fella, Stella!" he sang.

"Sure...*mom*... I can do that for you," I said, trying to sound conversational to convince Malice that I was in fact talking casually to my mother. "But, mom, uh, you know I don't like broccoli, and I've already cleaned up my room...what's that? No, mom, those aren't my cigarettes in the trash can. No, I *don't* know whose those are...oh, just great! Well, excuse me for living! But...but...damn it, mom! Why are you being such a...no, no I didn't mean that...yes, you know I do...you *know* I do...me too, okay, I'm sorry too. Love ya."

"Nicely done, Stella," the voice said to me. "It sounds like you and your mother have some serious issues you need to work through. Perhaps some family counseling when this is all over? I'm just throwing it out there."

"What do you need me to do?" I glowered at the voice through the phone.

"This is what I want from you. Please listen closely, and take copious notes. Now, I don't want to hurt your mother. Actually, I kinda *do*—she is somewhat of a pain in the ass, no offense. Not to mention incredibly expensive to feed. I'm sure I'm not telling you anything you don't know already. Anywho, if you want her to remain unharmed, I need you to do something for me. I need you to come to her house in Phoenix. *Alone*. Your vampire friends must know nothing about this. If Edweird found out about this he'd come down here and slap me around like there's no tomorrow...um, forget I just said that. Anyway, there will be further instructions when you get here. Did you get all that, Stella? I'll now open up the phone lines for any questions. Anyone? Anyone? Okay then, I'll see you soon. Now, say good night, Stella, and hang up the phone."

"Good night, Stella." I said and hung up the phone.

Malice had entered the room and looked at me. "Everything okay with your mom? Sounds like things are pretty normal, and that all is well. Am I correct to conclude this, or is there anything you'd like to fill me in on?

"How dare you, Malice!" I bellowed. "You just ended your sentence with two—count 'em—*two* prepositions! Could you *be* any more inconsiderate of my feelings?"

Poor English does not usually disturb me that much, but my mother's kidnapping was greatly upsetting me. Moreover, I was starving and I had no idea of the address of the Chinese restaurant where my carry out order was waiting and getting cold. This was not a good day for me. Not a good day at all.

"You need not get upset, Stella." Malice said reassuringly. You'll be safe as long as you stay here. And we'll make sure that your mom is also safe and sound and well fed. And I'll take some English classes at Sporks Community College to correct my language deficiencies if that will help to put you at ease."

"That all sounds great," I said distractedly. "Hey Malice, can I write a letter to Edw…, uh, my mother, for you to give to him—HER—the next time you see him, HER?"

"Sure thing, Stella. There's an unopened box of stationery in the kitchen. It was free with every purchase of a family sized box of Life cereal. You can use that to write your letter to Edw..., er, your mom."

"Thanks."

After stopping dog/pig from humping my leg as I entered the kitchen, I found the stationery in a kitchen drawer. Next to it was a box of Crayola crayons. I grabbed the one called "Midnight Blue" and began to write.

Dear Edweird,

Hi! How are you? I am fine...No, I can't lie to you. I am the opposite of fine—I am NOT fine! If you get this letter, then I am dead. If you don't get this letter, then I am also dead. So, to sum it up, I'm pretty much dead as a doornail. But if by small chance you happen to get this letter and I'm not quite dead yet, please don't come after me. And what I mean by that is, get your fine ass over to me, pronto!

Ya know...I don't blame you for this mess I'm in. But seriously, if it weren't for you and your Draculian friends, I'd probably be living a normal life right now. So you do the

math—which might be a problem for you since you're like, what, a hundred years old and still in high school? What's up with that, seriously? Well, it was nice knowing you.
Hugs and kisses.
Stella.
P.S. If you happen to run into Shame, break his legs for me.

I shoved the letter into an envelope and left it for Malice. With Shame now calling the shots and out for blood—*my* blood—my untimely demise seemed inevitable. I stood little chance of surviving an attack from a vampire. How I wish I had a lethal weapon to protect myself. If only I had a gun, or easy access to one. If only a completely clueless paternal family member were issued a firearm as part of his job. If only.

14. DITCH THE SULLENS

BY EARLY NEXT MORNING I was desperate to leave the Sullen compound and get to my mother. The night before I pleaded with the Sullens to let me go, but they refused. We did, however, come to a compromise. We would all drive down to my mother's house in Phoenix; that way they could still protect me, and still look after my mother—that is, *if* she was still alive. If we happened to find her dead, the Sullens offered to help me find a piano box to bury her in. I thought that was awfully sweet of them.

Edweird would not be joining us on our road trip to Phoenix. He had already left town the day before for God only knows what reason. However, he did make plans to fly into Phoenix about the same time that the rest of us would arrive. Before he left Sporks he had gone back to the Fantasy Forest to retrieve the Partridge Family's abandoned, psychedelically colored bus for us to travel in. Remarkably, it looked and ran as good as it ever had. The Sullens also believed that in this bus we could travel interstate inconspicuously. I started to wonder if vampires were colorblind.

My stomach was aching from anticipation, and though I hadn't eaten yet, I barely had an appetite. But I needed to keep up my strength, so I forced myself to drink some orange juice and eat a piece of toast with jam. And a couple of eggs, sunny side up. A side of bacon, a stack of waffles no less than four inches high, a half dozen sausages, some more bacon, a side of hash browns, a box of instant grits, a stick of butter to coat my stomach, and a bowl of freshly canned fruit salad in extra heavy syrup. I remembered that my mother had a name for all this: She called it her "snack."

It was fast approaching 8:00 a.m., the time we agreed to leave for Phoenix. I was showered and shaved well before then, and my clothes were neatly packed into a small Scooby-Doo suitcase I had borrowed from Harley. The Sullens had gone over the final details of our trip then calmly boarded the bus. Curiously, we all ended up sitting two to a seat, despite the fact that there were no less than 32 individual benches.

I won't bore you with the details of our trip. It was long and tedious. And after the thirteenth hour of "I Spy" I was ready to launch myself into oncoming traffic. But we made it to Phoenix safely, and in plenty of time to stop off at the airport to pick up Edweird.

Carpile parked the bus in a lot adjacent to the terminal for arriving flights. He waited in the bus while Malice, Casper and I went inside to pick up Edweird. We hopped on the moving sidewalk to our gate and I only fell twice, which was a personal best for me. Once we made it safely to the other side I figured that this would be my best opportunity to lose them. I immediately put my plan—"Operation Ditch the Sullens and Rescue Mom from Shame the Really Mean Vampire"—into effect. (I had thought up the name myself, with a little help from Casper.)

"Hey," I said in a playful voice. "Edweird's flight hasn't arrived yet, so how about we play a game while we wait. I got it—how about a game of 'hide and seek?' The two of you against me. Since you think you're such hot-shot tracking vampires, this should be no problem for you. But if you ask me, you got no game. A bunch of talk, constantly running your mouths. Seriously, you got nothin.' When you was born, the doctor told your mama, 'Congratulations, you just gave birth to *nothin'*!' The both of you are just wasting my time."

I suspected my trash talking would force Casper and Malice into this competition, if nothing else than to save face. They stared at each other then back at me. Casper was glowering like there was no tomorrow.

"Girl, if you can't shut your pie hole, then I'll do it for you. So, bring it on."

"Excellent." I said. "I'll hide, and you seek. You count to a hundred—no, let's making it challenging for you—a thousand, and we'll see how good you are. And if you mess up—which you will—you'll need to start over. Any questions?"

"No questions." Malice and Casper each said.

"Good, then let's get started. Ready? Go!"

I took off in a full sprint toward the nearest exit. I hadn't quite calculated my ground speed to coincide with the opening of the sliding glass doors, and crashed hard into them. I was temporarily knocked out, but quickly regained my senses, and stumbled my way outside. A line of cabs was waiting for passengers, so I hopped into the closest one.

"Get me to 415 S. Meyer Lane, and step on it. There's an extra twenty if you get me there in fifteen minutes."

"Yes, ma'am!" The driver said excitedly. He started the cab and quickly accelerated to 60 mph, running through the traffic signal that had just turned red a second earlier.

We arrived at my mother's house in about fourteen minutes. I paid the cabbie the toll displayed on the meter, and true to my word, slipped him another twenty pesos. He glowered at me, mumbled something in Pig Latin, and sped away. I ran to the front door of the house, mistaking it for an automatic sliding door one might find in an airport, and again crashed head first. I only briefly lost consciousness, and was able to come to my senses in less than a minute. I pulled myself up and rang the door bell. No one answered, so I reached for the emergency key duct taped right below the door knob. I opened the door, pausing briefly before I entered. I slowly peered inside and was somewhat surprised to find that the place appeared completely undisturbed and looked rather normal to me. I didn't know what else to do besides sit down on the couch and wait for further instructions.

About two minutes later I heard loud static from Harley's old CB radio in the spare bedroom. I walked in and saw the radio in the middle of a table. Then a voice came through.

"Breaker 1–9. I'm looking for a young filly, handle name 'Stella' from the Southwest state, to get on the horn. Do you copy? Over."

I picked up the handset, pressed the side button, and replied. "This is Stella. What's the handle on your end? Over."

"This is Vamp-1. You need to get yourself over to the House of Glass pronto. Do you read me? Over."

"Roger, I copy that, Vamp-1. My ETA is ten minutes. Over and out."

My encounter with Shame was about to begin. One of us would not make it out there alive. Ain't that a shame?

15. THE HOUSE OF GLASS

THE HOUSE OF GLASS was an old arts and crafts studio that had gone belly-up during the Great Sand Shortage of '94. The building remained as a kind of landmark in the Scottsdale downtown area. Fortunately, it was only a few blocks away from the house. The thought of having to get another cab, and dishing out even more dollars for a trip where I would likely be maliciously mauled to death, had, quite frankly, ticked me off. It's not like I would be getting my money's worth out of the ride. I was thus relieved by Shame's choice of a local venue for the upcoming massacre.

It was unseasonably cool for Phoenix this time of year, with temperatures dipping to just under one hundred degrees in the shade, so I didn't mind the walk. When I arrived at the House of Glass I noticed that the main door was open. I walked in, and as I suspected, the place was abandoned. As I went farther into the building I could hear a faint voice in the distance. I recognized the voice to be my mother's—or Rich Little's or Dana Carvey's. Or Shame, who, if nothing else, does an outstanding impersonation of my mother. My ultra developed brain told me it was Shame.

"Stella? It's your, um, mother. Come here Stella," the voiced called out to me.

I walked down the hallway and entered a large room where the voice was coming from. In the middle of the room was a six foot curtain suspended by two flag poles. Two marionettes were dangling by strings in front of the curtain. One was quite large with too much makeup. I assumed that one was supposed to be my mother. The other was dressed all in black, with dark hair combed back and shark-like fangs extending from his mouth; I figured that one was either Vincent Price, but more likely, Shame. The stage props, I must say, were poorly constructed, and I somewhat disappointed that the last theatrical performance I would ever see was so amateurish. But, I also realized that the production was put together on a limited budget and with significant time constraints. I, therefore, would withhold my comments until after the show.

"Stella, thank God you're here!" The fat marionette called out in my mother's voice. The marionette looked me up and down and said, "You're so skinny, Stella. Why aren't you eating? You know, boys like girls with some meat on their bones...and sweetie, maybe you should think of wearing something a little more feminine than those old blue jeans. It wouldn't kill you to put on a dress now and then, and maybe a little makeup, too? Just to bring out your pretty eyes."

"Christ, mom!" I shouted at the marionette. "Would you let it go already? I'm old enough to decide what I'm going to wear, what I'm going to eat, and who I'll date. Do you think you can drop it already?"

The other marionette watched in silence and simply rolled his eyes. Both of them took a bow and dropped to the ground forming a tangled mess. Then, from behind the curtain, Shame appeared, just as I suspected. But there was no sign of mom. I guess he couldn't find a crane big enough to haul her in. Thank God she was safe. What now became clear was that this whole charade was a trap, and *I* was the prey, not my mother. I figured this out myself. I have very strong deductive powers.

Shame glided over to me and stood just a few feet away. He had a calm look about him, the kind of look a calm vampire might have if he were acting normally. Then he immediately struck a pose, extending an outstretched arm high in the air with his finger pointed toward the sky. His knees were bent, angling toward the side as well. The whole routine was frighteningly reminiscent of John Travolta in *Saturday Night Fever*. I felt a bit nauseated.

"So, you've come, and you're alone," Shame said evenly, his steely eyes fixated on mine. "You follow directions very well, Stella. But you made this too easy for me. I was hoping that as my prey you would at least put up a fight. Clearly, this is not the case. It'll all be over before you can say, 'Check, please!'"

The whole time he was giving his speech he continued to strike poses. First, Madonna-like in which he framed his face with his hands, then like Marlene Dietrich in Ninotchka, and finally like Gloria Swanson in Sunset Boulevard. He stopped pacing at this point, turned to me with his eyes flaring and sang out, "I'm ready for my close-up Mr. DeMille."

Then he continued on, prancing about the studio and talking to me. "You are like a helpless animal—absolutely no threat to me. This hunt is nothing more than a restaurant dinner buffet. All you can eat. The entire meal is prepared and laid out for me to devour to my heart's content. Drinks $1.79. Tax not included. Children under three eat free when accompanied by a paying adult. Good food, great prices. A real good value."

"Why do you want to eat *me*?" I asked. "Is it because I am so juicy sweet? What is it about me that makes you want to you stick your pointy teeth into my pink flesh? How about a nice roast beef sandwich, side of fries, and a cup of soup? And as many trips to the salad bar as you like."

"Because you're Edweird's meal ticket—no pun intended." He chuckled. "And as sweet as you are, revenge is even sweeter. Devouring you would kill Edweird as well, and what a bonus that will be."

Everything Shame did and said was so matter-of-fact. There was no mystery as to how things would unfold—who would win, and who would die. He had nothing to fear. This was simply nature's food chain with a predetermined pecking order. He was the big pecker, and I was the peckee. I glowered at the big pecker.

"Any last requests, Stella?" he said getting right to the point.

I thought this out carefully, both to stall the inevitable, and to make my last deliberate act a memorable one. "Hmmm, last request, huh? I'd love to listen to the Beatles last live performance of *Sgt. Pepper's Lonely Hearts Club Band.* For my last meal I'd like a rack of lamb, a Caesar salad with dressing on the side, and for dessert a scoop of sorbet with raspberry sauce. Oh, and I'd like to make that 'to go.' Do you accept American Express?"

"That's just not going to happen, Stella," he said. He looked a little sheepish, and a tad disappointed. "The Caesar salad is made fresh daily, but with the dressing already on it. I can't put the dressing on the side. I wish you had called ahead and let me know your preferences."

"Ah, skip it. I'll pick up something at the airport later on today." I said. "No worries."

"I think you are missing the point, Stella. The only afternoon meal will be *you.*" He explained. "You smell so sweet, floral and lovely. Your hair is like silk, as is your silky smooth skin. Your lips are so soft and supple; I imagine that they, too, are luscious and silk-like. I can understand why Edweird is so drawn to you. He has excellent taste in fine human flesh, and all things of, or related to, silk."

Shame's eyes suddenly grew dark and narrow. For the first time I saw him agitated. The biological drive for human blood was overcoming him. He needed sustenance, and soon. I offered him one of my

Drake's Devil Dogs, but he politely declined. He didn't want to ruin his appetite. It was now just a matter of seconds before he would pounce and rip me to shreds, and then devour my lusciousness. I was hoping that he'd save me a drum stick before I passed out. Wait, that really didn't make any sense at all. I hate dark meat. What was I thinking? I was delirious with fear.

"Just one more thing, Stella, before I begin this fabulous feast. Things might get messy, and I want to be prepared for the worst." He reached inside his pocket and pulled out a neatly folded item. He then unfolded a very thin plastic bib with a picture of a large, red lobster.

"I'm such a messy eater. These things are life-savers," he said. "Saves me a trip to the cleaners."

He put the bib up to his chest and tied the two straps behind his neck. He then put his arms down to his side, and examined his protective garment. "I know it looks ridiculous, but hey, who's gonna tell?" He looked over at me and winked, and we both shared a hardy laugh together.

"Geeze, I'm really going to miss you, Stella," he said to me sincerely. "But now, it's chow time. Let the feast begin!"

I felt a rush of adrenaline surge through my body. The last thing I remember was seeing his arms extending high and wide in the air, his eyes narrowing to tiny slits, and his pointy white teeth glistening. Then everything went black. Well, things didn't actually *turn* black; it was my mind that went blank, which in effect, is like things turning black.

Six of one, half a dozen of the other. You get the point.

Nothing else to see here, people. Let's keep it moving.

16. THAT'S GOTTA HURT

I woke up, got out of bed, dragged a comb across my head. But I had no idea where I was. When I came to my senses I noticed that I had been lying on a hospital bed. How I got there, and what had happened, is both a mystery to me and to you. I can't wait to learn what happened. Let's read on, shall we?

I was not alone in the room. There were several chairs, a small shelf, a television secured to a stand hanging from the ceiling. A tiny dresser, lots of hospital equipment, a trash can, and a TV remote control. What else? Venetian blinds, some amateurish artwork, a metallic doorknob, a tiny guest room and/or closet, and if I'm not mistaken a colorless, odorless liquid beverage that I believed to be water. Oh, there were also some people in the room as well. First, there was Dr. Sullen, who was standing over me with a look of intense concern on his face. Or it might have been indigestion. Edweird was also there, crouching by my side, his perfect granite eyes piercing mine, which I found quite painful. And then there's Malice.

Before I could say anything a short man walked in the room wearing a white lab coat with a stethoscope around his neck. *Crazy outfit*, I thought to myself. Was I at some sort of costume party? After a brief moment, I deduced that he, in fact, was some type of real doctor. When he saw that I was awake he walked over to my bed and gave me a warm smile.

"Good morning, Stella," he said, "My name is Dr. Robert Smithjonesme. I'll be taking care of you."

"*Smithjonesme*? What the hell kind of name is that?" I asked, sickened by the thought that someone would have to spend his entire life with such a ridiculous sounding name.

"Oh, that. Well, my Father's surname is Smith, and my mother's maiden name was Jones. She didn't want to give up her name when they got married. So, my parents just kind of combined their names and gave it to me."

"And the 'me' at the end of your name? What's that about?"

"Who the hell knows?" He said, throwing up his arms and shaking his head despondently. "I think they just threw it in there to make it completely and utterly ridiculous."

"Mission accomplished," I agreed.

"Well," he continued, "I'm glad to see that you're awake and alive. I'll let you spend some time with your friends here. I'll be back later this afternoon to perform CPR on you. Until then, have a pleasant day."

Dr. Smithjonesme then walked out of the room. I sat up in my bed, and immediately a smile came to my face at the sight of the Sullens.

"Hi guys! What's up?" I asked the group.

"How do you feel, Stella?" Dr Sullen asked, sullenly.

"I feel...fine." I said, but began to realize that every inch of my body felt like it had been slashed by a wheat shredder then submerged in hot lava flowing down from Mount Vesuvius circa 418 A.D.

"I had the strangest dream. There was complete chaos, screaming and crying. Bodies were flying every which way. I tried to run, but couldn't." I suddenly got this sense of déjà vu. I looked at everyone in the room. "And *you* were there, and *you* were there, and *you* were there, too!"

"Oh, Dorothy, that was not a dream." Malice said. "You were involved in a terrible, terrible experience. We're so sorry."

"Wait a minute." I said, glaring at Malice. "Did you just call me '*Dorothy*'?"

"Um...no..." Malice said, quickly gazing over at Edweird and Dr. Sullen. I said, 'Oh, you *poor thing.*' Yeah, that was it. You know, you're pretty pumped up with drugs right now. I don't think your mind is too clear."

"Tell me about it," I said. "I have absolutely no idea what happened or how I got here. So, what exactly did happen to me? Anyone? Anyone?"

"I'll tell you the whole story, but I prefer to communicate through interpretive dance," she said.

"Please, no! I pleaded. "Can't you just use words?"

"If you insist." She said.

Phew.

Malice began. "After we discovered that you had ditched us at the airport we immediately went to your mother's house. Once we got there Casper picked up your scent and followed it to the House of Glass. We ran inside just in time to see Shame pounce on you. Edweird quickly pulled him off and pounded him senseless. Even after the beating Shame still had some life left in him so I kneed him in the groin a few times. Casper finally finished him off by plugging him with a .22 caliber pistol. There was blood everywhere—that's right, blood everywhere. Some of it was his, but most of it was yours. He messed you up pretty good, I tells ya. You were looking real bad."

"Oh my," was all I could say.

"We gave you first aid then loaded you in the car." Malice continued. "We then drove to hospital, stopping only for a Big Gulp and beef jerky, the extra spicy kind. Oh, Edweird wanted ice cream, so he insisted that we stop at the Dairy Queen, the king of ice cream in all the land. What'd you get there, Edweird, the Blizzard with chocolate chips and rainbow sprinkles? We used the drive-through to try to save time, but what a mistake that was! The line wasn't long, but I swear it did not move at all. I think the cash register may have been broken or something. Once we all got our desserts we hurried to hospital, and you were given lots of blood. You've been in and out of consciousness for three days now."

I closed my eyes, trying to envision all that had occurred. It was pretty much a blur to me.

"That's an unbelievable story." I said, shaking my head in horror and disbelief. "I've never had to wait more than just a few minutes at the DQ drive-through. Their service is on par with their outstanding food and ice cream. That's just so unlike them. What a nightmare that must have been for you."

"You have no idea, Stella." Edweird interjected. "There you were—the love of my life, my life force, my reason for living—knocking on death's door, and it was all my fault." Edweird stared intensely into my eyes, struggling to contain his emotions. "And on top of that, DQ screwed up my order! *Who* gets both chocolate chips *and* chocolate sprinkles?!? What a horror."

"The nightmare is finally over, for all of us," Malice said calmly. "The Shame and DQ disasters are behind us, and Stella here is on the road to recovery. I can see it happening."

Malice stared hard into my face, piercing my soul, my entire being, every atom that came together to make me *me*. A smile seemed to come to her slowly. It was a sad smile, just the same. She looked at me for a long moment, and then turned her gaze to the other Sullens in the room. Her expression was soft yet intense, as if she were trying to recall a Shakespearean verse she could recite that would appropriately capture the moment. Or she had terrible gas, and was ready to let one fly. Then, addressing everyone in the room, she delivered a stirring speech that would make the angels weep.

"One day, with a little luck, we will have our Stella back with us, completely healed and spiritually whole again. Soon—and with God's help—her oozing, grotesque facial scars will start to fade. Her one *good* eye will start to see colors again, and those unidentifiable shapes she now sees will start to have meaning. And her Mr. Potato Head-like left ear will look and smell less like rotten cauliflower and may start to detect actual sounds all around us. Elegant wigs will cover her hairless, scabbed-encrusted scalp. She will gracefully don custom-made glasses that her face can support even with her partial nose. Gold and wooden teeth will smartly replace the porcelain-like ones that once populated her mouth. And since she's never had much of a chin in the first place, the chin implant will actually *improve* the one she never had."

Malice slowly moved her gaze from my once lovely face down my body, as if she were caressing my wounds under the bandages. She started to become a little emotional, as did everyone else in the room. She continued her assessment, ignoring any and all information that the team of medical specialists had predicted for me.

"In time, her body will grow tired of rejecting every skin graph surgically attached to her, allowing her to heal from the third degree burns she received when Casper spilled his steaming hot cocoa on her on the way to the hospital. One day, she will learn to grasp objects, even without the existence of an opposable thumb—um, make that *thumbs*. Long, attractive fake fingernails will extend beautifully from the stubs where her fingers once were. Silicone implants will restore her bust line to a feminine shape far more appealing than the concave chest she has now. A beautiful, flowing dress will smartly veil what's left of her shredded left leg and her right wooden pegleg as well. And the gangrene stench emanating from her remaining toes will one day remind us of home, and the time we discovered that Edweird had accidentally left out the blue cheese while we were on vacation. Oh yes, we will warmly welcome Stella back to our house again—every leap year when February 29th falls on a Sunday."

Tears began to well up in my eyes, causing an incredible burning sensation due to the exposed nerve endings where my bottom eyelashes once were. "You all are so wonderful. I love you so much. Dr. Sullen, you are like the father I never had. Malice, like the sister I have always yearned for. Casper, you are like a brother who would always protect me, and steal money from my purse only when it's absolutely necessary."

I turned to Edweird, my good eye straining to make out his form. After a long two seconds, I added, "And Edweird, you are like the star quarterback, captain of the chess team, four-time pinewood derby pack champion Michael Jenner, super hero and super villain, Yin and Yang, Abbott and Costello, Cain and Abel, Venus and Serena Williams, Josh and Drake, and the 1945–1953 New York Yankees all rolled up into one. *That's* how special you are to me. Oh, and the 1992 Superbowl Champion Washington Redskins, who really should go down as one of the greatest professional football teams of all time. Them, too."

I again focused my good eye at the Sullen family. It suddenly struck me how each one of them was such a perfect form. Through hundreds of years, and countless physical challenges and emotional hardships, they somehow had kept themselves looking so beautiful, and so perfect. *How was this possible*? Surely, they must have injured themselves from time to time, either through battle or perhaps smashing their car while driving intoxicated. What kept them looking so fine, so free of unsightly scars and blemishes, after all these years?

Then I remembered something I had read about vampires in the book I had read months ago, *The Idiots Guide to Vampires, Werewolves, and Investing in International Stock and Bonds.* Vampires have the ability to heal themselves, no matter how serious their injuries, to their perfect pre-injured state. Of course, it all made sense now. I felt my heart began to pound loudly and I began to smile for the first time in days. I had just discovered a way to make myself whole again.

"Hey," I said to the Sullen family. "A crazy thought then entered my mind. If I were to somehow become a vampire, would all these wounds kind of heal themselves? Would I start to look like the old me, but *better*? And if this were the case, and I did become a vampire, could I move in with you guys? I know this all must sound pretty insane, but I think we should consider making this a reality."

At once the Sullens all turned even paler than they already were, which I didn't think was possible. They quickly glanced at one another, reading each other's thoughts as they liked to do. Their expressions remained intense until Dr. Sullen spoke on behalf of the family.

"Um, uh, well…hmmm…how can I put this…uh, um…hmmm. Well, yes and no. Mostly yes. Actually, well, yeah, you are completely right. We vampires do heal ourselves. That's how we keep looking so spectacular all the time. But regarding your other question—about moving in with us—well, you know, our house is kind of full right now, and no one has plans to move out any time soon. And we have only one working toilet. So, if you did somehow become a vampire you'd have to live in a Motel 6 or something, pretty much forever, and that can be pretty pricey. And Stella, you must realize that there are so many other problems with what you are suggesting, you just can't imagine."

"So, what is it you're trying to tell me, Dr. Sullen?" I asked. "What do you think I should do?"

"Well, since you've asked me a direct question, I'll give you my honest opinion. I think that once you get out of this hospital, you should start a completely new life—as a lonely elephant woman at a circus sideshow attraction. Maybe marry a gimp, and start a family of equally freakish offspring. How's that sound to you, Stella?"

Dr. Sullen waited anxiously for me to nod my approval. When he saw my hesitation, he tried to offer up addition information that would help seal the deal.

"Of course, the less desirable alternative would be to transform you into an unbelievably beautiful vampire who would live in a magnificent house next to ours with her true love for all eternity. But what quality of life would that be?"

The Sullen kids, listening very intently to Dr. Sullen, all nodded in agreement. Dr. Sullen's words had given me so much to think about. On one hand, I could make my current family so proud by following in my mother's footsteps and becoming a circus sideshow freak. And remember, my mother was the Tri-States largest woman at the Phoenix circus when she met her true love—or at least the man who only occasionally steals money from her bank account. But on the other hand, spending eternity with my true love didn't seem half bad. Not bad at all. Something I could probably learn to tolerate, and perhaps one day enjoy. I had so many mixed emotions running through me. I so needed a stiff drink.

"Well, I was just thinking out loud about this whole vampire thing," I said. "I don't want to invite myself where I'm not really wanted."

"Exactly! You hit the nail right on the head, Stella," said a relieved Dr. Sullen. "And speaking of head, you better lay yours down and get some rest. Doctor's orders!" He pulled a grayish leech out of his coat pocket and dangled it at me, as I backed away willingly.

The Sullens all gave a collective sigh of relief, and their normal alabaster skin tone had returned to their faces. Malice suggested that they all raid the hospital's blood bank to celebrate my not moving in with them, and that she was buying the first round. They all quickly filed out of the room. Edweird, who was last to leave, turned to me and said, "I'll see you soon, babe. And hey, don't go changing to try and please me. I love you just the way you are."

"Thanks, Edweird." I said, and watched him leave the room.

I turned the TV on to the Dr. Phil show. Today's episode: "My father is a vampire, and he married a no good stinkin' werewolf." Not five minutes into the show I fell asleep. When I awakened the TV was off and the room was empty, except for Edweird. He was sitting in a chair next to my bed, so completely focused on his connect-the-dots magazine that he didn't notice my shuffling.

"Damn," I heard him mutter to himself, "This shouldn't be so friggin' hard."

"Edweird, you're still here? What time is it? Where is everyone?"

Edweird's eyes peered over his magazine and directly in to mine. "My family up and left. They got pretty bored, and frankly, you don't really smell that good. It's 9:30 a.m. Pacific Daylight Time. And, yes, I'm still here. Duh."

"Of course you're here, Edweird. You're always with me, right when I need you the most."

Edweird shot me a slight smile. "That's what friends are for. Yup, just friends. Just good ol' chums, close buddies. *Super* friends, that's what we are. Yeah."

I sat up in my bed. His comment disturbed the crap out of me. *Friends*? Is that what we were? I guess that I had no idea what our relationship was all about. And now, with all that had happened, I had no idea what the future might hold. To sum it all up, at this particular point in my life, I was just pretty damn clueless. It was time to take a stand.

"I don't understand you, Edwerid. You're a mystery to me. When we first met you seemed to hate me. Then you warmed up a bit, but soon turned cold. Then burning hot. Then a little spicy, but that became cool like a refreshing mint—a Junior Mint. And now, after all that's happened, all you want to be is just friends again. I just don't get it."

Edweird's eyes widened as if he had just seen a ghost, and then narrowed again. "For crying out loud, Stella," Edweird said passionately, "have you seen yourself lately? I mean, I don't want to sound so superficial, but you're kind of hideous looking. It's hard for me to be in the same room with you without losing my lunch. I haven't fed in a week just so I don't spill my guts when I see you. So, please don't blame me for wanting to put the brakes on our relationship, at least until I can look at you without wanting to gouge my eyes out."

The insensitive bastard was right. Listening to his biting words helped me decide right then and there exactly what I was going to do. Although the calling of the circus sideshow would be hard to resist, I had to take the other path. One way or another, I would become a vampire, or die trying. Once we figured out a way to make this happen, nothing would stop us from being together, forever. I couldn't wait another second to tell Edweird.

My declaration to Edweird would have to wait, however. The silence of the intensive care unit was abruptly interrupted by some kind of ruckus coming from the hallway. I couldn't identify the source of the disturbance. However, I was able to overhear two nurses talking excitedly to each other.

"Could it be? Is that *her*? I had heard that she had eaten herself into total oblivion, and was completely bed ridden," the first nurse said.

The other nurse replied, "I had heard the same thing, but Dr. Smithjonesme told me she'd dropped five hundred pounds and was now suffering from anorexia."

"It's hard to know what to believe. Besides, what would the largest woman in the Greater Phoenix/Tri-State area—a major celebrity and true American hero—be doing here?"

"Beats me. Maybe she's visiting a friend. Who knows?"

Then I heard heavy footsteps marching down the hall. They were heading in this direction. A woman's voice was bellowing out,

> *You'll be swell!*
> *You'll be great!*
> *Gonna have the whole world on the plate!*
> *Starting here, starting now, honey, everything's*
> *coming up roses!*

My fractured jaw dropped to my chest. A second later my mother stomped in the room, ending all mystery about what was going on.

My mother's body mass had increased from *enormous* to *gargantuan and beyond*. Since I last saw her, she must have put on an additional two or three hundred pounds. Clearly, the allure of the circus sideshow was just too much for her to resist. And as her weight increased, so did her fame and fortune.

She had become a true celebrity in her own right. Only in America!

Though I hadn't seen her in many months, I still felt closer to my mother than anyone else in this crazy world. She was the only person I could tell my deepest, darkest secrets to. Sure, she abandoned me for some schmuck she had met only a month earlier. And even though she threw me out of the house to live with my estranged father in a two-bit town, I still loved her very much. I was also hoping to inherit a large sum of money from her when she died at a relatively young age from her morbid obesity.

My mother nearly fainted when she saw me. "Stella! My poor Stella! Who did this to you? Was it that boy…what's his name…Edweird?"

Mom then spotted Edweird quivering in a chair next to me. Without a moment's pause she thundered over to him, her eyes shooting daggers into his. Edweird looked like he had just seen the devil—an enormous one—and tried to flee. But even with her tipping the scale at pert near half a ton, mom was too fast for him. As Edweird was vacating his chair, she used her gorilla-like arm like a club, making contact with his head and knocking him to the ground. After watching her prey fall, she plopped her entire being on top of him. The room was filled with the sound of Edweird's cracking ribs.

"Mom, no!" I shouted. "Edweird saved me. He's the hero here. You've got to believe me."

Mom pulled out a turkey leg from under her Moo-Moo, took one giant bite big enough to feed a family of four, and turned to me.

"Well, I don't like him, not one bit. But if it wasn't him, then you need to tell me who did this to you. Nobody puts baby in a hospital bed."

"Mom, it's best you don't know." I said. "I'll fill you in about my life on a need-to-know basis. It works for Harley, and I think it's best for you."

"Don't you go telling me what I need to know and what I don't need to know," she protested. "I'm not leaving until I get the whole story from you. I've got plenty of time. I can wait."

"Fine. If you must know, then I'll give you the *Reader's Digest* version." I said. "A vampire named Shame was pretty ticked off that I hoarded all the Cal Ripken, Jr. autographed bats at the Sullen's baseball game. So he tricked me into coming down to your home in Phoenix to protect you. Then he ambushed me. But Edweird, along with his 100 year-old sibling vampires, saved my life before I was completely devoured. Next thing I know I'm waking up in this hospital bed. That's it in a nutshell. God's honest truth."

Mom stared at me for a long moment. She was examining my face for any signs of deception. She knew I had never lied to her in my entire life. Our relationship was built on trust, and a single lie would irrevocably rattle its foundation. I gave her no reason to doubt me.

"You've been drinking again, Stella. I can smell the alcohol on your breath. I just hope you get some help before you kill yourself. That's all I've got to say. Goodbye."

Using all her might, my mother managed to heave herself off Edweird, and without even looking

at me, paraded out of the room. Even after the sound
of her departure disappeared which was quite awhile
considering the thundering her thighs alone made, I
could still hear her singing:

Honey, everything's coming up roses and daffodils!
Everything's coming up sunshine and Santa Claus!
Everything's gonna be bright lights and lollipops!
Everything's coming up roses for me and for you!

"That was weird," Edweird said in the under-
statement of the decade. "You're mom's a real
sweetheart, and I can also see where you got your
good looks."

"She's all I got, Edweird. That is, besides *you*.
Which reminds me, Edweird, I need to tell you
something very important. It's about my future
plans—*our* future plans. I'll let you know up front
that I've already made up my mind. But you must
promise me that you won't say anything at all until
I'm done. Can you do that for me, honey?"

"Hmm," Edweird said, looking a bit uneasy.
"This should be interesting."

"Come closer to me, Edweird. I want to whisper
this into your ear so no one else can hear."

Edweird limped over to me, holding his cracked
rib cage as he struggled to breathe normally. He leaned
his head down next to mine, so that my lips were nearly
touching his ear. I took a deep breath, paused for effect,
then began telling him my plans for our future. For the
next thirty minutes, using flow charts, graphs, and
advanced statistical modeling, I explained how our life
together would unfold. Edweird listened intently to my

presentation, resisting the urge to question the road map I had laid out for us. When I finished saying what I had to say, Edweird quietly stood up and smiled sweetly at me. He reached out his perfect hand and gently caressed my imperfect cheek. He tried to speak but no words left his mouth. Then he politely excused himself to use the facilities, and quickly darted out the room. That was the last time I ever saw him.

Well, you win some, you lose some. Such is life. Hey, I wonder what ol' Yakob's been up to. He seems like a sweet guy. Maybe he and I will hook up one day. You never know.

EPILOGUE

I learned the truth at seventeen,
That love was meant for beauty queens
And high school girls with clear skinned smiles
Who married young and then retired.
- Janis Ian, *At Seventeen*

THE LARGE DISCO BALL was brilliantly lighting up the school gymnasium, where the boys and girls from Prozac High, dressed in tuxedos and ball gowns, were dancing cheek to cheek. This was the first end-of-the-year high school dance I had ever attended. A group of my girlfriends and I decided that there that were enough positive things going on for us to celebrate. I, for one, felt whole again. Miraculously, all my wounds had healed completely. And I felt emotionally stable. I had put the whole humongous mom, retarded dad, and vampire boyfriend fiasco behind me. Heck, stranger things have happened to me—but don't get me started on that. Besides, my best buddy Yakob was around to help me through these difficult times. He also let me borrow one of his motorcycles because my truck had up and died.

I didn't end up dancing too many times that night. During my first dance I twisted my ankle pretty badly while trying to do a pirouette. After a couple more dances my ankle swelled up like a watermelon on steroids. So, the remainder of the night I spent talking to my friends and rejecting every boy who asked me for a dance. That kind of turned me on, if you want to know the truth.

Maria and I also spent a lot of time discussing our summer plans. Since neither of us had any jobs lined up, we decided the best thing for us would be to get away for a while. Maria told me how she missed her family back in Italy; they lived in a small town that seemed to be a popular place for international tourists.

"You know what, Maria?" I said. "I think you should visit your family in Italy this summer. And I think you should take me along. I could use a vacation, and I have quite a few extra dollars to my name. When Edweird ran out on me he left his wallet behind, and that boy would always carry a large wad of cash. So, as far as I can see, nothing is holding us back."

"Oh, Stella! I am so happy to be going home!" Maria yelled out, unable to contain her giddiness. "My family will love you, I'm sure of it. And you will love them, too. I can't wait to call Grandma

Volturi, and tell her that her granddaughter and Stella are coming home to spend the summer in Volterra!"

The evening had started at twilight and now it was getting late. There was a rumor going around that an eclipse was forthcoming. It better hurry, because dawn would soon be breaking.

I walked over to Yakob and gave him a great big bear hug. He put his arms around me and we started to gently sway. The sleep deprived DJ announced the name of the last song of the evening, *New Moon*, which he said was a big hit when he was growing up in the 1950's.

"Doesn't he mean *Blue* Moon?" Yakob asked.

"Yeah, I think he does," I said. "But you know what? *New Moon* sounds pretty perfect to me."

The end.

Printed in the United Kingdom by
Lightning Source UK Ltd., Milton Keynes
141109UK00001B/30/P